Jennifer,

Thank you for all the inspiration and encouragement !

I hope you enjoy the read .

Very best ,

Sara

NANNY FAMILIES

Sociology of Children and Families series

Series editors: **Esther Dermott**, University of Bristol, UK and **Debbie Watson**, University of Huddersfield, UK

The Sociology of Children and Families monograph series brings together the latest international research on children, childhood and families and pushes forward theory in the sociology of childhood and family life. Books in the series cover major global issues affecting children and families.

Forthcoming in the series:

Social Research Matters:
A Life in Family Sociology
Julia Brannen, November 2019

Designing Parental Leave Policy:
The Norway Model and the Changing Face of Fatherhood
Elin Kvande and **Berit Brandth**, March 2020

A Child's Day:
Children's Time Use in the UK from 1975–2015
Killian Mullan, July 2020

Sharing Care:
Equal and Primary Caregiver Fathers and Early Years Parenting
Paul Hodkinson and **Rachel Brooks**, November 2021

Find out more at

bristoluniversitypress.co.uk

NANNY FAMILIES

Practices of Care by Nannies, Au Pairs,
Parents and Children in Sweden

Sara Eldén and Terese Anving

BRISTOL
UNIVERSITY
PRESS

First published in Great Britain in 2019 by

Bristol University Press
University of Bristol
1-9 Old Park Hill
Bristol
BS2 8BB
UK
t: +44 (0)117 954 5940
www.bristoluniversitypress.co.uk

North America office:
Policy Press
c/o The University of Chicago Press
1427 East 60th Street
Chicago, IL 60637, USA
t: +1 773 702 7700
f: +1 773-702-9756
sales@press.uchicago.edu
www.press.uchicago.edu

British Library Cataloguing in Publication Data
A catalogue record for this book is available from the British Library

Library of Congress Cataloging-in-Publication Data
A catalog record for this book has been requested

ISBN 978-1-5292-0151-2 hardcover
ISBN 978-1-5292-0154-3 ePub
ISBN 978-1-5292-0152-9 ePdf

The right of Sara Eldén and Terese Anving to be identified as the authors of this work has been asserted by them in accordance with the Copyright, Designs and Patents Act 1988.

Cover design by blu inc, Bristol
Front cover image: kindly supplied by Lumina @ Stocksy
Printed and bound in Great Britain by CPI Group (UK) Ltd, Croydon, CR0 4YY
Bristol University Press uses environmentally responsible print partners

Contents

List of Figures

Acknowledgements

Our deepest gratitude goes out to all you nannies, au pairs, parents and children who so generously invited us into your world, your homes and your rooms, and shared with us your narratives of everyday life in nanny families. We have been entrusted with your stories and, while sewing them all together has not been easy, we sincerely hope that our efforts to treat your narratives with respect will be visible to you when reading this book. To each and every one of you, we give our warmest thanks.

We are indebted to many colleagues and friends for providing support and encouragement, and for asking intellectually provoking questions, during the four years that we have conducted this study. Åsa Lundqvist has been our closest 'critical friend', always ready to share her immense knowledge, as well as a glass of wine, when necessary. The members of the research environment 'Family, Migration, Welfare', as well as students and staff at the Department of Sociology, Lund University, have followed us from start to end. Their expertise, advice and support have been crucial on so many different levels. We particularly want to thank our dear friend and colleague Agneta Mallén.

This study has also brought us new friends. Lise Widding Isaksen and Lena Näre invited us to be part of the international research environment 'North-Eastern Care Chains', which provided us with critical support, as did the Nordic network 'Significant Others'. Esther Dermott and Janet Fink came to visit in Lund, and their enthusiasm and encouragement made us believe that we could actually write a book. We have had the opportunity to present this study at many different venues, both academic and public, and we are thankful for all the constructive feedback that has been shared with us.

Hayley Davies generously provided office space for writing at the University of Leeds in the autumn of 2017. On top of that, Hayley offered her critical eye in reading the final draft of some of the chapters, as did Catrine Andersson, Lars Eldén, Dalia Mukhtar-Landgren, Christine Roman and Johanna Sixtensson – for this, we are very grateful. Thank you Anna Lidskog for excellent transcription work, and Erik Nylund who visualised our data.

The Swedish Foundation for Humanities and Social Science generously funded this research, and the Swedish Institute guesthouse in Kavala provided much-needed space away from home for writing and analysis work.

Finally, we give our most personal thanks to the people who have been our everyday supporters throughout these years, who have been 'doing care' together with us: Oscar, Måns, Hillevi and Max; and Martin, Elise and Alina.

1

Introduction: Nannies, Au Pairs, Parents and Children in Sweden

Nannies and au pairs in *Swedish* families? Really? The initial reaction when we began our research study some years ago was often surprise. One might have heard of Swedish girls going to the UK or US, or maybe France, in the gap year between high school and university, but who comes to work as an au pair in Sweden? Are there nannies in Sweden? Are not all Swedish children taken care of by publicly funded daycare centres?

Indeed, signs of there being nannies and au pairs employed by Swedish families had occurred earlier. In the beginning of the 21st century, a number of scandals unfolded in the Swedish media regarding the use of domestic care workers in certain high-profile well-off families, testifying to the actual prevalence of these groups. In 2006, the media reported that two women MPs in the newly elected Conservative–Liberal government had hired several domestic workers over the years, including nannies and au pairs, all undeclared and at very low pay. The Conservative Party leader, Fredrik Reinfeldt, soon to be prime minister, had also hired au pairs, it was reported. The scandal – which included the testimonies of former nannies and au pairs about harsh conditions of working in 'posh' families in upper-class areas – led to the MPs resigning from their positions, less than two weeks after their commencement. Fredrik Reinfeldt's use of au pairs, however, was found to be within the rules of the Migration Agency and of no liability to him becoming prime minister.[1]

A couple of months later, in the beginning of 2007, this newly elected government presented their first reforms. One of them was a tax deduction for domestic services, such as those provided by cleaners and nannies. The problem, according to the government, was clearly not the use of the services, as such, but rather that they were too expensive.

This was the reason why people turned to the informal market if they wanted to employ cleaners, nannies and au pairs, just as the two fired MPs had done. By making the informal market formal, it was argued, several problems could be solved (Bill 2006/07 no. 94).[2] Work opportunities for the unemployed could be created, thought to be especially suitable for migrants and other groups having a hard time getting into the labour market. Most importantly, the lack of gender equality in Swedish families, prevailing despite decades of family politics promoting the equal sharing of work and care responsibilities, could be solved. The use of domestic services was no longer thought to be an exception to the ways in which families worked out their 'jigsaw puzzle of life',[3] as it is popularly called in Sweden, that is, the managing of everyday life demands from family and work. Instead, the government proposal suggested that this should become a legitimate way of doing family.

Swedish parents have for many decades delegated care to actors outside of the family as most Swedish children are enrolled in publicly funded daycare institutions. However, since the 1960s, and following the ideals of gender equality, the care work taking place in the private sphere was to be shared between mothers and fathers (Lundqvist, 2011). Of course, privately organised alternatives have always existed, such as informally paid babysitters, or neighbours and mothers helping each other out (Gullestad, 1984). However, never before has there been a private, formal and also state-supported market for domestic care services in Sweden. Furthermore, this formal market is paralleled by another growing market: the much more informal practice of hiring au pairs. When more and more families have the opportunity to, and choose to, hire nannies and au pairs to take care of their children, everyday life changes.

Families are what families do. This simple, but rather revolutionary, insight of family sociologist David Morgan (1996) in proposing his concept of *family practices* some decades ago has opened up the field of family studies and enabled new empirical, methodological and theoretical developments within the field. However, one type of 'doings' around, to and in family settings has largely been missing in family studies: the doings of paid domestic workers. Maids, nannies, au pairs and cleaners all carry out practices that can be – and in most families still are – done by family members, such as serving a child an afternoon snack or cleaning up in the kitchen after dinner, and they do so in the setting of private homes. In addition, their doings of these chores can be argued to affect the doings of 'ordinary' family members. When a nanny or au pair becomes responsible for preparing and serving that afternoon snack, this affects both adult and child family members' everyday lives. It allows, for example, the adult to be absent for longer periods of time, and it relieves him or her (though it is, according to statistics, mostly her) of some of the feeding work that family life entails (DeVault, 1991; Anving, 2012). For the child, it means the presence of a new and often quite important person in everyday life.

While paid domestic work has been overlooked in family studies, it has been thoroughly researched elsewhere, most importantly, in research on *global care chains*. This research strand starts out in the identification of the retraction from care work of First-World women, who move into paid labour markets, which has led to new labour market opportunities for – often migrated – women entering different vocations of paid care work in the homes of middle-class families (Hochschild, 2000). However, while global care chain research has thoroughly investigated the working conditions of migrant nannies and au pairs, and sometimes also focused on the relationship between employers and employees, less attention has been given to the ways in which domestic workers, and especially nannies and au pairs involved in care for children, experience everyday care in families. Most remarkably, while parents', nannies' and au pairs' perspectives have been included in several studies (see, for example, Macdonald, 2010; Lutz, 2008, 2011; Bikova, 2017), and while a few – and important – studies have contributed with the perspective of children 'left behind' when Third-World mothers leave to take care of children in First-World families (Parreñas, 2001, 2005), very little attention has been given to children who *receive* this form of care (for exceptions, see Spyrou, 2009; Souralová, 2013, 2015, 2017). By also including these children's perspectives, this book will provide new and important insights into the study of nanny and au pair care in families.

In this book, all three categories of actors involved in the practice of 'doing nanny/au pair care' will be heard and listened to: the parents hiring nannies and au pairs; the nannies and au pairs themselves; and, finally, the children who are taken care of by nannies and au pairs. Together, these actors create the opportunities for and engage in what we call *care situations*: the spaces and times in everyday life in which nanny and au pair care happens. The three categories of actors are involved differently in these situations: the parents are the ones enabling them through their decision to invite nannies and au pairs into the family; and the nannies and au pairs are the ones answering this call, and the ones trying to live up to the parents' expectations of 'good nanny care'. However, most importantly, the nannies, the au pairs and the children are the ones finding themselves directly within the care situation; in their everyday encounters during the time they spend with each other, mostly without the parents being present, they 'do care'. The different positioning of these three categories of actors has motivated the disposition of this book: the parents, the nannies and the au pairs, and, finally, the children get their perspectives presented, each in their own chapter.

We will argue throughout this book that care in itself is *simultaneously* a practical and emotional activity – in fact, distinguishing between the two aspects is impossible – which makes the capturing of the care situation a delicate matter. To do this, we have used innovative methods such as diaries and drawings, trying to move beyond the taken for granted, and to get at the, sometimes invisible, doings of care. This theoretical and methodological pursuit will be the focus of our next chapter. However, before that, we wish to give the reader a more thorough introduction to the context for the study: the Swedish welfare state and the different – and in some respects unique – care solutions that have been developed here throughout the 20th century. The overall aims and ideals of how care for children should be organised historically and up until today will be in focus, looking in particular at the different roles of private and public solutions, and at the ways in which paid domestic work has historically figured in Sweden.

Care in the Swedish welfare state

In theorising on different forms of welfare states, Sweden and other Nordic countries are usually identified as belonging to the 'universal caregiver model' (Fraser, 1994; Esping-Andersen, 1999), in which the state explicitly aims at making it possible for men and women to combine caring and earning, and where the two endeavours are – ideally – equally shared. Norwegian sociologist Arnlaug Leira (1994) has argued that the Nordic countries can best be described as 'caring states', meaning that the state has historically offered a social security system for all, as well as high-quality care for those in need. This means that in terms of care, '[t]he emergence of the welfare state meant a renegotiation of the boundaries between the public and the private, between the state and the family, and between citizenship and charity', resulting in interventions by the state into parts of the private sphere (Leira, 1994: 196). The fact that the state has been responsible for some parts of care for dependants sets the Nordic welfare states apart from other European countries, where these needs have historically been viewed as an individual responsibility left to private charity, provided by other family members or by voluntary organisations. However, this does not mean that care is totally collectivised in the Nordic countries; rather, it is a partly public and partly private responsibility, where borders between the two are not settled once and for all.

Early times: women, paid labour and the work–care dilemma

Ever since the beginning of the expansion of the welfare state in the 1930s, the overarching aims of Swedish family policy has been to promote social and – later on – gender equality (Borchorst and Siim, 2008; Lundqvist, 2011, 2017). To fight poverty and decreasing fertility rates, the family became an important policy area for state interventions (Lundqvist, 2011: 130). The period between 1930 and 1950 was characterised by great improvements in people's living standards and a number of reforms directed towards women in their position as carers, such as free antenatal clinics, child welfare centres and general childcare allowances. Still, the underlying ideal of these family policies was that of a male breadwinner (Hirdman, 1989; Lundqvist, 2011: 38).

When an increasing number of middle-class women started to enter the paid labour market, the hiring of a maid became a practical solution to solve the work–care dilemma of these women (Öberg, 1999; Platzer, 2006). At the beginning of the 20th century, working as a maid was considered a good vocation for young girls from rural areas. In a governmental investigation concerning domestic work in 1937, the domestic worker was regarded as a needed worker. However, it was also stated that privately organised domestic work was already soon to become unnecessary as, it was argued, it should be replaced by state-funded collective solutions (Lundqvist, 2007: 129–30; Calleman, 2011). After the Second World War, as other work possibilities in, for example, the expanding industrial sector emerged, domestic work became a less attractive job for Swedish women. As a response to this, and to ensure that there would still be a good supply of domestic workers for Swedish families, labour market regulations were changed to make it easier to recruit migrant labour. This resulted in an influx of, in particular, German girls who came to Sweden to work as maids (Strollo, 2013).

During the 1960s, there was a great need of workers in Sweden due to the booming economy, expanding industries and a growing public sector. This resulted in women entering the paid workforce to a much greater extent than before. Between 1960 and 1980, the percentage of women in the labour force in Sweden grew from 38 per cent to 83 per cent (Lundqvist, 2017), and has stayed around this figure since then (Statistics Sweden, 2016). A major concern at this time was how children should be cared for when women left for work. The former privatised solutions of maids and nannies were deemed insufficient, and the solution suggested was public daycare (Myrdal and Klein, 1957; Sjögren, 2003). As early as in the 1930s, Alva Myrdal argued that all children should be taken care of by educated workers in public daycare, and that this was an investment in the children's future and in social equality (Myrdal and Myrdal, 1934). Her ideas were not realised at the time, but they reoccurred in later decades, coupled with new ideological ideas: the fight for public daycare became part of the fight for gender equality and women's rights in the growing women's movement of the 1970s (Schmitz, 2007; Lundqvist, 2017). Public daycare has since gone from involving few children in the 1960s to expanding remarkably in the 1980s and 1990s, and today enrolling almost all children: in 2016, 84 per cent of all Swedish children between the ages of one and five years were in daycare (Swedish National Agency for Education, 2017). Attending daycare is increasingly seen as a normal part of childhood and is generally regarded by parents as a positive and important part of children's upbringing (Swedish National Agency for Education, 2013). The motives underpinning the expansion of public daycare were both gender equality and social equality: it made it possible for women to work outside of the home while simultaneously ensuring quality care for all children, regardless of parental income (Björnberg, 2002; Ahlberg et al, 2008; Sandin, 2012). Today, the fee for daycare is dependent on parental income, with a maximum fee of approximately €130 per child per month (Swedish National Agency for Education, 2017).

With the expansion of public care institutions, paid domestic workers became an increasingly unusual category of workers. At the beginning of the 1970s, the legislation on domestic work was changed through the instigation of the Domestic Work Act 1971. While some improvements were made, this Act was weaker compared to other labour laws, for example, allowing for more overtime and dismissal without cause. The need for separate labour legislation for this kind of work was motivated by arguments of its special character as it was being carried out in the homes of other people. In the preparatory works for the Act, it was once again stated that domestic work in private homes was an arrangement of the past, and that it would soon be replaced by public collective solutions for all (Calleman, 2011: 126).

Consolidated gender-equality policies and remaining practices of gender inequality

In the 1960s and onwards, the concept of the gender-equal family was firmly established in Swedish family politics. The debates were focused not only on how to further support women entering the labour market, but also on making men take on more caring responsibilities. This led to a change of focus: from *women only* to *parents* and *parenthood* (Lundqvist,

2011; Johansson, 2014). In 1974, maternity leave was transformed into the gender-neutral *parental* leave, representing a major change on both a practical and discursive level as it could now be used by both mothers and fathers. The caring father was in focus (Sandin, 2012: 197), culminating some decades later in the 'daddy quota' of the parental leave (in 1995), designating one month out of the parental leave that could not be 'given' to the other parent (Klinth, 2002; Ahlberg et al, 2008). More 'daddy months', as they are popularly called, have been added, and in 2019, three out of the total 16 parental leave months have to be used by the other parent. The fact that family policy explicitly included fathers was regarded as a 'double emancipation', further weakening the male-breadwinner model and moving towards a dual-earner/dual-carer model, enabling not only women's participation in the paid labour force, but also a sharing of work and care responsibilities between men and women (Lundqvist, 2011: 72).

The reforms have resulted in the labelling of Sweden – and other Nordic welfare states – as 'women friendly' and 'state feminist' (Hernes, 1987: 153). However, the fact that gender-equality policies were being promoted by the state did not transfer easily into actual practices. The question of how to fully realise the ideal of gender equality remained unresolved, and the gaps between ideals and practices became the focus of feminist critique (see, for example, Borchorst and Siim, 2008; Ellingsaeter and Leira, 2006).[4] Research shows that gendered practices and separate norms of what motherhood and fatherhood should be still remain (Ahlberg et al, 2008; Roman and Peterson, 2011; Anving, 2012). Regardless of family constellation, women are still the primary caregivers; they do most of the care and housework, and particularly so in families with small children. They take the main part of the parental leave, and they more often stay at home when children are ill. Women also work part time to a much larger extent than men. They earn less, and the labour market in Sweden is also highly segregated; women work to a considerably greater extent within the public care sector, and men are more often in managerial positions (Grönlund and Halleröd, 2008; Klinth and Johansson, 2010; Boye et al, 2014; Statistics Sweden, 2016).

The lack of correspondence between gender equality as an ideal and as a practice has led to new discussions on how to solve the work–care dilemma. The idea to counter women's doing of 'double shifts' (Hochschild and Machung, 1989), through introducing a tax deduction for household services, was first suggested at the beginning of the 1990s. The idea was met with great scepticism and was followed by heated debates where especially the Social Democratic Party positioned itself strongly against it. The debate was labelled 'pig-debatten', the 'maid debate', and the use of the subservient term 'piga' served to mark the suggestion as un-Swedish and as belonging to the past, to a 'clear and visible class society with masters and maids in people's homes' (Kvist, 2013: 215). The suggested reform was not introduced at this time, but the discussion continued and gained new interest in the coming decades.

Neoliberal challenges and a growing market for paid domestic work

In 1991, the Conservative–Liberal government proclaimed "'a freedom of choice" revolution', resulting in no restrictions on for-profit daycare providers in Sweden, which challenged the general public daycare system and led to a growth of private (as well as parent cooperative) daycare institutions (Brennan et al, 2012: 383).[5] This change went hand in hand with what has been labelled 'the turn to parenting' (Daly, 2013), stressing parents' responsibility in making the right choices for their children, and this being decisive for the future of children and of society (Halldén, 2010; Gillies, 2011; Sparrman et al, 2016; Littmarck, 2017). Coupled with the failure of fully realising the dual-earner/dual-carer ideal, this can be seen as paving the way for the introduction of the tax deduction for household services, and, later, the growth of the nanny and au pair market.

The debate on tax deductions for private household services in the 1990s was revived before the election in 2006, when the Conservative–Liberal Party coalition promised to initiate such a reform if they came into power. When they entered government in 2006, the so-called 'RUT tax deduction'[6] was one of the first reforms to be introduced. In the preparatory work of the tax deduction, the focus was on the customers and their needs, and very little attention was given to employees' working conditions (Calleman, 2011: 128). The reform meant that purchasers of domestic services such as cleaning, nanny services and gardening work were allowed to deduct 50 per cent of the labour costs from their taxes. While the debate was intense at first, with time, the RUT deduction has become more accepted and even embraced by some of its former political opponents, most importantly, by the Social Democrats (Kvist and Peterson, 2010; Carbin et al, 2017).[7]

The main arguments for the reform were: first, that it would formalise an informal market; second, that it would create jobs for people in 'hard-to-employ' categories, such as newly arrived migrants and people with low education; and, third, and most importantly, that it would have a positive impact on gender equality (Kvist and Peterson, 2010).[8] According to quantitative research, the hiring of domestic workers has led to a reduced pay gap between men and women among women in middle- and high-income jobs (Boye et al, 2014). At the same time, critics have pointed towards the reform's different consequences for different groups of women: while some have been released from parts of care work, others are positioned in precarious and low-paid employment (Gavanas, 2010; Kvist and Peterson, 2010; Kvist, 2013; Eldén and Anving, 2016). In addition, the tax deduction has meant a shift in people's attitudes towards buying domestic services, which is a more common and acceptable way of solving the work–family dilemma today (Eldén and Anving, 2016; Carbin et al, 2017).

The nanny and au pair market in Sweden

The RUT tax deduction and the growing acceptance of employing private domestic care workers has enabled both the occurrence of a new market for nannies, organised by nanny agencies, and also a parallel and more informal market of au pairs. 'Global care chains' have occurred in Nordic societies (see, eg, Isaksen, 2010; Näre, 2016), visible in the emergence of an au pair market, which has been studied in Denmark (Stenum, 2010, 2015; Liversage et al, 2013), Norway (Stubberud, 2015; Bikova, 2017) and Finland (Wide, 2017). In Sweden, the focus of research has primarily been on the growing market for cleaning services (see, for example, Platzer, 2007; Gavanas, 2010; Kvist and Peterson, 2010; Gavanas and Calleman, 2013; Kvist, 2013), and, with a few exceptions (Calleman, 2010; Gavanas, 2013), the nanny and au pair market has not been studied up until now.

The nanny market

The tax deduction for household services has led to a huge growth in the formal market for domestic services. In 2016, the total amount of the RUT tax deductions was €340 million, compared to €25 million in 2009 (Swedish Tax Agency, 2017). Most tax deductions are claimed by households of high economic standing, and the major part of the deduction is for cleaning services (Statistics Sweden, 2015); however, the market for nanny services is growing rapidly (Dagens Industri, 2017).

Nannies working in Sweden in the formal market are employed by agencies.[9] The majority operate in and around the wealthier areas and suburbs in Stockholm, but agencies are established in all the bigger cities in Sweden, such as Gothenburg, Malmö and Uppsala, and most of their customers are double-income, upper-middle-class couples.[10] The largest nanny agency in Sweden, Nanny.nu, employs over 1,400 nannies, and their turnover was €2.5 million in 2016 (Nanny.nu, 2018).

The agencies do not employ anyone full time, but rather by the hour. The agency is involved in the matching procedure between the family and nanny, but, thereafter, arrangements regarding working hours and tasks are negotiated between the parents and the nanny. The cost for hiring a nanny is around €16–20 (after the tax deduction), and the nanny is paid €9–11 per hour before tax.[11] Few agencies adhere to collective agreements with unions in negotiating compensation, which means that the nannies' pay is regulated solely by the agencies and the market. Most of the nannies in our study report working two to three afternoons per week and about three hours each shift, and their main responsibilities are defined by the agencies as caring for children.

The au pair market

Parallel to the growth of the formal nanny market, a more informal and invisible market of au pairs has emerged and expanded in Sweden. The reason for this invisibility is that different rules and regulations cover different groups of au pairs. Au pairs coming from countries outside of the European Union (EU) have to apply for a work permit to work as an au pair (if in Sweden legally) and are thereby visible in statistics. However, au pairs coming from within the EU are not visible in statistics due to the European agreement of free movement of labour. This invisibility also means that it is very difficult to assess the actual size of the market. Previous research, mainly based on contacts with au pair agencies, calculated that the number of au pairs in Sweden rose from almost non-existent at the beginning of the 1990s to around 3,000 by 2010 (Platzer, 2006; Calleman, 2010). Our study – although qualitative – indicates that the market has grown considerably over the last ten years: interviews with parents attest to a growing prevalence and acceptance of hiring au pairs, and interviews with au pairs report an increase in both the number of families looking to hire au pairs and the number of au pairs seeking placement in Swedish families. This is further supported by observations in social media groups for au pairs and parents. Similar developments have been identified in other Nordic countries: research in Denmark and Norway shows that the number of au pairs has been growing steadily there too.[12]

For those applying for a work permit for au pairing, the rules from the Swedish Migration Agency state that: the au pair must be between 18 and 30 years old and have no accompanying children; the workload is limited to care for children and 'light housework' and must not exceed 25 hours a week; the au pair is also expected to study Swedish (with tuition paid by the host family)[13]; and work and studies combined must not exceed

40 hours per week. The minimum wage is €320 per month before tax, including food and lodging (Swedish Migration Agency, 2017).

Since Sweden has not signed the European Au Pair Agreement, au pairs from within the EU are not regulated by specific rules, but instead fall under the general regulations for EU workers. This, in turn, means that, in theory, the Domestic Work Act (enacted in the 1970s and discussed previously) applies to EU au pairs, meaning that they are considered as workers, not as being on cultural exchange.[14] However, this is generally not known of by any parties involved; instead, the guiding principles referred to by both parents and EU au pairs in our study are the same as the ones stated by the Migration Agency, defining non-EU au pairing.

Outline of the book

Since the 1930s, social and gender equality have, to various degrees, been major principles for the expansion of the Swedish welfare state and its organisation of care. However, opportunities to outsource parts of the care work in the private sphere have led to new ways of organising family life, parenting and care, for those who can afford them. Within this context, we ask: what happens to the doing of family and care when nannies and au pairs enter Swedish families? To analyse this, we need to zoom in on everyday practices of care and include narratives of all the actors involved in the care situation created in families hiring nannies or au pairs: parents, nannies, au pairs and children. To be able to do this, we need to, first, in Chapter 2, present the theoretical backbone of the study, most importantly, discussions of the concept of care in feminist theorising, as well as in global care chain research. The *emotional activities* in care are at the centre, and we also situate our study in relation to childhood and family studies, arguing for the need to see children as co-constructors of the care situation, as well as to see the gains of moving beyond the taken-for-granted when taking one's point of departure in a family practice perspective. This chapter also presents the research study upon which the data for the book are based, and the different methods (interviews, diaries and drawing methods) used to encourage participants to reflect upon and talk about everyday practices.

In the subsequent three chapters, we present for the reader the narratives of the different actors who are participants in nanny and au pair families. Chapter 3 focuses on parents and looks at their views of how family life changes when nannies and au pairs are hired, primarily related to issues of gender equality and 'good parenting'. We zoom in on parents' expectations of the nanny and au pair: what they want her to do for the family and in relation to the children, as well as how they frame her presence – is she primarily an employee, or more like 'part of the family'? In Chapter 4, we turn our gaze towards the nannies and au pairs. Here, we focus on their understandings of the work they do and the discrepancy between it being described as 'simple' and 'easy' and their experiences of demanding practices. We will also look specifically at their accounts of being in care situations with children, and of forming and breaking relationships with specific children. Finally, we will turn to their accounts of their position in the family, how they narrate their position between being an employee and 'part of family', and how this is related to a sometimes precarious work situation. Chapter 5 presents the narratives of the children: their understandings, and experiences, of the presence of nannies and au pairs in their everyday lives. The children's complex views of the care situation that they form with nannies and au pairs will be discussed, pointing towards both the possibilities – and necessities – of care as the basis of close and specific relationships, and the problematic framework interfering in this, through the constant break-ups with nannies and au pairs. Together, these three chapters make possible the highlighting of diverging and corresponding views on, and experiences of, the care practice in nanny and au pair families.

This is brought together in Chapter 6, where by recognising the gap between the expectations and experiences of nanny and au pair care, we identify the different processes through which paid domestic childcare becomes invisible. In conclusion, in Chapter 7, we address the need for studies of family practices to include paid domestic care in the analysis of 'doing family', as well as for global care chain research to problematise the concepts of 'care' and 'family'. This enables a critical analysis of new ways in which inequalities are done, within and between families, in today's changing welfare societies.

Researching Families and Paid Domestic Care

Exploring key concepts and understandings

Theorising care as labour and emotion, and beyond

When parents decide to hire a nanny or an au pair, when someone decides to take upon themselves the position of nanny or au pair in a family, and when a child is presented to a nanny or an au pair, the central activity that all parties expect to take place is *care*, more precisely, care with children in focus. However, care is a complex and contested concept, both for people engaged in the practice, as we will see in the upcoming chapters, and also for scholars researching it.

The theorising of care was the front line of feminist sociological research in the 1980s. The discussion was primarily concerned with finding ways of theorising gender and care, and especially unpaid care performed by women as wives and mothers, within the perimeters of the home. One analytic dichotomy became particularly important in this endeavour: the division of care into *labour* and *emotion*. Janet Finch and Dulcie Groves's (1983) classic anthology, *A labour of love: Women, work and caring*, was a starting point for a number of insightful contributions focusing on the need to distinguish between *caring about* and *caring for* someone. The general argument, put forward most clearly by Hilary Graham (1983), was that 'caring for', which is the labour part of caring, is too often conflated with 'caring about', that is, the emotional part of being fond of or loving someone, resulting in the hard labour involved in caring becoming invisible. This labour is often carried out by women. To understand the subordinate position of women, in family and in society as a whole, the analysis needed to take its point of departure in care. A theory of care needs to adhere to and include an acknowledgement of both the material and emotional aspects of care as caring is, as Graham (1983: 29) argued, 'experienced as a labour of love'.

At approximately the same time, care was debated outside of sociological research as well, most prominently in the 'ethics of care' debate in the fields of feminist psychoanalysis (Gilligan, 1982), feminist political science (Sevenhuijsen, 1993; Tronto, 1993, 1998) and feminist philosophy (Ruddick, 1990; cf Mason, 1996). One important contributor in this debate was Joan C. Tronto, who proposed an understanding of care as involving a range of different types of *activities*. Caring about, she argued, means 'listening to articulated needs, recognizing unspoken needs, [and] distinguishing among and deciding which needs to care about', and caring for is the phase of assuming responsibility to meet the needs that have been identified (Tronto, 1998: 18). From Tronto's perspective, the line between emotion and labour is blurred as 'thinking', 'feeling' and 'doing' become bound up in each other around the moral practice of care.

This idea was further developed by sociologist Jennifer Mason (1996) in her chapter 'Gender, care and sensibility in family and kin relationships'. Mason suggested that although the dichotomies of labour–emotion and care for–care about had served important purposes for the furthering of theorising and research at the time of their instigation, they were now increasingly inadequate. Despite acknowledging the necessity of both emotion and labour, as set out in Graham's argument, the sociological debates too often left the emotion part of the dichotomy unproblematised and under-researched, and instead turned towards a material and ideological reasoning, 'a kind of political economy of care' (Mason, 1996: 18). Mason (1996: 27) argued for the rejection of 'the idea that feeling, thought, mind, or emotion are inner, natural, essential states or essences of self', and proposed that thinking and feeling are activities, and, as such, a significant part of care.

Mason suggests new concepts for understanding care in family and kin relationships, most importantly, care as *sentient activity*. Examples of sentient activities, coming out of her own and others' empirical work on care, are '[A]ttending to, noticing, hearing, being attuned to, seeing, constructing, interpreting, studying, exercising an interest in the needs, health, wellbeing, behaviours, likes and dislikes, moods, individuality, character, relationships of specific others or thinking through, working out, organizing, planning, orchestrating relationships between oneself and others relationships between others' (Mason, 1996: 27).[1]

These activities are a significant part of doing care, often demanding and gruelling, but rarely acknowledged and often underestimated, even by the people who are themselves doing it (DeVault, 1991; Anving, 2012). Sentient activity is also obviously *activity*; while Mason is not suggesting that sentient activity is all there is to care – care is also often hard physical labour – she dismisses the dichotomy of labour–love on the grounds that it signifies activity only with respect to the first part of the dichotomy. Further, to talk about 'love' as the emotional part of care wrongly associates caring with positive feelings: care is by no means without conflicts and power relationships (Wærness, 1984; Tronto, 1998).

From the 1990s onwards, several critical voices were raised towards the care debates of the 1980s, often by the same researchers who had initiated the debates in the first place. Graham (1991), for example, identified two major problems that severely limit the analysis coming out of this research strand: first, the narrow focus on caring as the 'unpaid work of those who are related to each other through birth or marriage'; and, second, that 'caring is seen as all about gender' (Graham, 1991: 68). Taking upon herself the challenge of black feminist writers in Great Britain and the US, she called for a reassessment of foundational concepts and assumptions of theorising on care, taking into account the importance of 'race' and social class. Interestingly for our study, she made her argument through the case of domestic work, arguing that by primarily focusing on home-based kin care and by overemphasising gender, feminist care research – including her own work – had obscured 'other forms of home-based work and the social divisions which are inscribed in them' (Graham, 1991: 74). Tronto (2002) raised similar concerns and gradually started to develop broader concepts of care, and thereby to detach it from association with family and kin relationships. Like Graham, Tronto directed her empirical attention to domestic work, specifically, to the moral implications for feminists of the increased occurrence and use of domestic workers (Tronto, 2002, 2010).

Paid domestic care, global care chains and inequalities

From the late 1990s and onward, Graham's and Tronto's calls for a broadening of the care scholarship was in many ways met by the growing focus on paid domestic care work within the research field of *global care chains*. While the existence of paid domestic care workers is in no way new, as we, for example, saw in the discussion in the introductory chapter of early welfare state Sweden, the global care chain researchers argue that new parameters are visible today. The term 'global care chains' was first suggested by Arlie Russell Hochschild, who defined it as 'a series of personal links between people across the globe based on the paid or unpaid work of caring' (Hochschild, 2000: 131), such as when a middle-class woman in a rich country, often a mother with dependent children, hires someone to do the domestic duties that she herself cannot (or does not want to) do as she otherwise often finds herself having to work a 'second shift' in addition to her work on the paid labour market. This 'other woman' comes from a poorer household, and increasingly from a poorer household in a poorer sending country. The migrant domestic worker, in turn, may very well leave behind a family of her own, which, in turn, creates the need to find yet others (mostly women) to care for the domestic worker's own family (Yeates, 2012).

Research within the global care chain field has been cross-disciplinary and intersectional at its core, gathering researchers from different disciplines and perspectives, weaving together theories of migration, ethnicity, class, gender and labour, as well as, to some extent, theories of care. Due to its focus on the geographical movements of care workers, it has often put *migration* at the centre of analysis, which means that domestic workers of all kinds have been of interest, not only or necessarily workers involved in care for other human actors (for a critique, see Macdonald, 2010: 7). However, care is an inevitable part of almost all domestic work, regardless of its being explicitly stated in job descriptions (Anderson, 2000: 15), which led Hochschild to argue that 'love and care' has become 'the new gold': 'love is an unfairly distributed resource – extracted from one place and enjoyed somewhere else' (Hochschild, 2002: 26, 22).

Three interrelated theoretical assumptions about care are recurring in this strand of research. First, the *labour–emotion dichotomy* is central and, in large part, draws on the previously discussed contributions within feminist sociology, adding some dimensions specific to the situation of paid domestic care. In her classic contribution *Doing the dirty work?*, Bridget Anderson (2000: 116) warns against conflating labour and emotion, which 'can lead to an argument that care is not exploitative because women want to do it'. In paid domestic work, this dichotomy further plays a crucial role in reproducing the idea that one part of care – the labour part – can be bought as a service on the market, while the emotion part can be 'kept' by the employing party (Anderson, 2000: 119). A similar argument is put forward by Dorothy E. Roberts (1997: 51) of the division of labour into 'spiritual' and 'menial' housework, where the former is 'valued highly because it is thought to be essential to the proper functioning of the household and the moral upbringing of children', and the latter is 'devalued because it is strenuous and unpleasant and is thought to require little moral or intellectual skill'. While these ideas are certainly used in legitimising the buying of domestic services, in practice, the separation is not maintained. Employers are rarely 'looking for a labourer when they are looking for a carer: they want somebody "affectionate", "loving", or "good with children'" (Anderson, 2000: 119; see also MacDonald, 2010). At the same time, the dichotomy can still be used to disrupt the relationship between carer and cared for, if an employer so wishes: since 'real care' is assumed to be 'non-commodifiable', this relationship can easily be broken without consideration of the 'worker's feelings for their charges' (Anderson, 2000: 120). The power to define when paid domestic labour is 'just labour' or when it should also entail 'emotions' is in the hands of the employer in this respect.

In addition, several studies of paid domestic work also acknowledge the impossibility for domestic workers themselves to, *in practice*, disentangle care as emotion from care as labour. In Anderson's words:

> As anyone who has been involved with a child can tell, it is often through interaction on the level of basic physical chores – nappy changing, feeding, cleaning, that one develops a relationship with a young child ... caring requires 'face-to-face interaction' – that is, at the very least, relating. If this face-to-face interaction is repeated on a daily basis in the kinds of conditions experienced by many domestic workers, particularly those who live in, it almost inevitably develops into a relationship. The paid worker loves the child, the child loves the worker, and jealousy and family friction result. (Anderson, 2000: 120–1)

The labour–emotion dichotomy is thus identified as both *an argument reproduced by employers when it benefits their position* (to argue for their own continuous importance in the life of their children, to argue for their right to disrupt carer–cared for relationships, to argue for the conflation of the two when asking for an 'affectionate' care worker), and as *a dichotomy that does not correspond well with the actual practice of doing care work*, from the paid domestic worker's perspective, as it is argued that, in practice, the disentanglement of labour from emotion/love is not possible (Hondagneu-Sotelo, 2002: 86).

The second, and related, theme running through research on paid domestic work is the tension between being *an employee* and being *part of the family*. This is particularly the case in studies of care for children, and even more so when the care worker lives together with the family, as did all au pairs in our study. It also, as we shall see in the subsequent chapters, occurs in our conversations with all the actors of Swedish families hiring nannies and au pairs. The dichotomy builds on another well-known (and problematic) dichotomy, that of the private and the public. It is by 'slipping between the two imagined domains of the public and the private that the employer consolidates much of her power', Anderson

(2000: 5) argues, continuing: '[T]he worker may be treated as "part of the family" (governed by customary relations) when it is a matter of hours and flexibility, and as a worker (governed by civic relations) if she becomes too sick to work'.

The gradual incorporation of workers into families enables employers to see the domestic worker's labour increasingly as 'acts of love', and a move away from the simple, contractual bonds of employment towards the complex networks of kinship. In addition, it is common that domestic workers also strive for this position, at least in the beginning, since having a good relationship with one's employer is extremely important in the highly individualised working situation of working in a family (Anderson, 2000: 123). However, the (ideal) reciprocity of family relations will not arise as relations in paid care are always asymmetrical. Empirical research attests to employers being unwilling to consider the workers' own private lives, as well as to the many ways in which the 'part of the family' argument is used for extracting more labour out of the domestic worker by arguing that it is a 'family responsibility' to 'help out' or appealing to her love for the person(s) in her care (Anderson, 2000: 123; Búriková and Miller, 2010).

The third significant theoretical theme focuses on the different ways in which paid domestic care reproduces *inequalities between women*, inequalities related especially to *race/ethnicity* and *class*. This was, as we saw earlier, an important part of the criticism that feminists theorising care brought upon themselves in the wake of black feminist challenges. Returning to Roberts's (1997: 51) dichotomy of spiritual and menial care, this division is, she argued, inherently raced and classed: spiritual care is associated with 'privileged white women' and menial work with 'minority, immigrant, and working-class women'. Anderson presents numerous examples of how 'difference' related to race and class is done and reproduced between women, and argues that the association of domestic work with the body makes it 'dishonourable' and 'dirty': not having to do domestic work becomes a symbol of status (Anderson, 2000: 142). In this sense, domestic work defines women in a fundamental way: when the employer is buying the domestic worker's service (in Anderson's argument, her whole 'personhood'), the domestic worker becomes part of a 'reproduction of the female employer's status (middle class, non-labourer, clean) in contrast to herself (worker, degraded, dirty)' (Anderson, 2000: 2).

Research on children and paid domestic care

Very few studies have included children's perspectives on care in general, and paid domestic care in particular. This is, indeed, not surprising given the overall reluctance in social science to involve children in research. However, the 'new social studies of childhood' perspective has questioned conventional ways of looking upon childhood and children (Prout, 2005), and stressed children's agency and the importance of including children in research (Christensen and James, 2008; Eldén, 2013a; Davies, 2015). Studies of children and care that have included children's own 'voices' have, for example, challenged dominant views of children and childhood as a time free from work and characterised by play (Sandin, 2012) by pointing to the many ways in which children are involved in doing care. While most of this literature has reproduced the labour–emotion division of care discussed earlier (Morrow, 1996; Samuelsson, 2008; Nilsen and Wærdahl, 2014), some studies have shown that children are intrinsically involved in reciprocal activities of feeling and thinking, constituting care in personal relationships (Brannen et al, 2000; Brannen and Heptinstall, 2003; Seymour, 2005; Ridge, 2007; Marschall, 2014; Eldén, 2016). The reciprocal element in these studies is crucial; through highlighting the ways in which children are not only recipients of care, but neither, of course, only providers of care, they bear testimony to the ways in which children are part of *the care situation* created around them.

The dominant assumption in global care chain research is that children 'left behind' are the 'losers' of the global care chain equation, while children on the 'receiving end' are considered as the 'winners', the ones 'getting the caring gold' extracted from the poorer countries to the richer ones (Hochschild, 2002: 26). While acknowledging that individual children can, indeed, benefit from this arrangement, Tronto (2002) draws attention to the potentially negative moral consequences for children – and for society at large – when children are cared for by paid domestic workers. The family, she argues, can be seen as the 'ethical root' of a democratic society, and the presence of 'servants' counters the democratic ethos (Tronto, 2010). Children being cared for by nannies 'come to expect that other people, regardless of their connection to them, will always be available to meet their needs', and start treating 'people as mere means, and not as ends in themselves', which will foster undemocratic citizens, Tronto (2002: 40) argues. Studies that have actually talked to children about nanny/au pair care confirm Tronto's argument in some respects, showing, for example, how children can adopt racist attitudes towards domestic workers; however, they also point towards other, more complex, consequences (Spyrou, 2009). For example, Adéla Souralová's (2013, 2015) study of Vietnamese immigrant children and their Czech nannies showed the possibilities of close and mutual relationships also developing in paid private childcare. Souralová (2013: 154) stressed the daily mundane presence of nannies as a requirement for the development of a relationship characterised by 'mutuality, reciprocity, and emotion'.[2] There are, we argue, strong reasons to further investigate the experiences of children 'on the receiving end', and to fully acknowledge their participation in the care situation that is created in families that hire nannies and au pairs.

Studies of family practices

Some of the criticism directed towards feminist sociologists' theorising on care can also be directed towards the research field of family sociology: there has too often been a too singular focus on nuclear family relationships. However, recent developments within the field open up new possibilities for the analysis and theorising of relationships in and 'beyond' family and kinship.

Several theoretical approaches, emerging from the mid-1990s and onwards, developed out of a shared frustration and discomfort with the existing framework as being stuck in an uncritical reproduction of the family: the nuclear, heterosexual, parent–children relationships situated in the home. The frustration with this model came both out of a recognition of its normative force and, most importantly, through growing awareness of its inability to capture lived relationships and experiences. To develop theoretical models that could better capture the 'fluidity and complexity in modern life' (Morgan, 2011: 52) has been a shared concern in several theoretical approaches, including the 'family practices' approach (Morgan, 1996, 2011), theorising on intimacy (Jamieson, 1998), personal life (Smart, 2007; May, 2011), family configurations (Widmer and Jallinoja, 2008) and displaying family (Finch, 2007; Dermott and Seymour, 2011).

The approach of *family practices*, introduced by David Morgan (1996) in his book *Family connections*, has been the most influential of these approaches and inspired multiple new ways of researching and theorising on families and relationships. Morgan searched for a concept that could capture fluidity and process: 'doings' rather than 'beings'. Family practices, Morgan (2011: 5–7) argued, implies:

1. a 'linking between the perspectives of the observer and the actor', meaning that compared to when researchers use the noun 'the family', there is often incongruence with the actual ways in which family lives are lived and experienced;
2. a 'sense of the active', giving 'doings' central stage and allowing for a 'whole set of what appears to be trivial or even meaningless activities

[that] is given meaning through its being grouped together under one single label, that of family';

3. a 'sense of the everyday', meaning both life events that are experienced by many (partnering, parenthood, etc) and also 'those activities which seem unremarkable, hardly worth talking about';

4. a 'sense of fluidity', which has two dimensions: first, fluidity in boundaries, whereby family activities can include and exclude, as who 'counts' as a family member is not fixed; and, second, that any set of practices described as family practices can also be described in other terms, such as 'gendered activities' or care activities; and

5. a 'linking of history and biography', meaning that 'individuals do not start from scratch as they are going about family living'; there is 'structuration' in practices shaped by legal, economic and cultural constraints.

Family is thus constituted and reconstituted through constant everyday doings: 'Family practices are not simply practices that are done by family members in relation to other family members but they are also constitutive of that family "membership" at the same time' (Morgan, 2011: 32).

This, then, poses the question of whom we define as a 'family member'. Morgan acknowledged the difficulty in this question, and the risk of the reproduction of notions of the family as a noun, as members of some designated collective. However, the fluidity in the definition (point 4) opens up a possibility of getting around this: 'The practices, including not merely what is done but also how it is done, define who counts as a family member, at least for the time that these practices are being followed' (Morgan, 2011: 10). This fluidity, then, makes possible an inclusion of, for example, a nanny or an au pair as 'part of the family', a defining practice that is, indeed, recurrent. At the same time, a family practice perspective also accounts for 'stability' in the concept: the social and historical 'structuration' of 'family' shapes the doings. As we will argue later in this book, the 'doings' of nannies and au pairs are 'doing family' in the families they work for, but in ways that often leave the contribution of nannies/au pairs in this doing invisible as they are not 'really' part of the family.

The most important way in which the family practice perspective contributes to our study is the weight it gives to *activity* and *everydayness* as constitutive of family. This corresponds very well with Mason's (1996) concept of care as sentient activity, which shows how care is, indeed, an everyday emotional *activity*. The family practice perspective further adds to this by making it possible for us to investigate the ways in which care doings, done by different actors, are constitutive of 'doing family'.

Towards an integrated understanding of nanny and au pair care in families

The scholarship of global care chains has been tremendously important for the sociological and feminist theorising of care, pointing out its classed, raced and heterosexist bias, as well as its problematic focus on the gendered relations as being formed solemnly in the women–men dichotomy. It has pointed to other ways in which 'the family' and 'the home' are unequal and, indeed, sites of exploitation, and it has allowed for the voices and experiences of paid domestic workers to be heard. However, with a few exceptions, it has largely accepted and reproduced the dichotomy of care as labour–emotion, often also assuming emotion to be equated with 'love'.

This untangling of labour from love is, in one sense, logical and necessary in global care chain research, just as it was in early feminist analysis of women's unpaid work at home: it shows the hard labour of caring carried out by domestic workers. However, as discussed earlier with reference to the early work of Tronto (1993) and, most importantly, Mason (1996), there are shortcomings of this dichotomy: as we will show throughout the book, important dimensions of nanny/au pair 'care doings', emotional doings that are also sometimes part of the 'exploitative' nature of domestic work, are, indeed, missed if we stick to the simple dichotomy of labour and emotion, and if we conflate emotion with love.[3]

We will further show that the discursive position of nannies and au pairs as being either 'part of the family' or 'employee' is inadequate. Through acknowledging their doings of everyday care – in activities that might seem 'trivial or meaningless' – we can also analyse how they are part of new and unequal, and often invisible, ways of 'doing family'.

The study and its methods

The study upon which this book is founded, 'Care for children in an era of private market services: A study of nannies, children and parents',[4] set out as a primary objective to capture the complexity of *practices of caring* in Swedish families employing nannies and au pairs, which meant two things: listening to the perspectives of all participating actors (nannies, au pairs, children and parents); and making use of practice-focused methods to get at the often invisible doings of care in everyday life.

Entering the field

Our entrance point to researching family practices in 'nanny families' was through nannies and au pairs. They were the first to be interviewed in the project, followed by parents and, finally, children. The nannies were all recruited through nanny agencies. This way of contacting nannies could potentially mean that our sample is skewed, that is, that we only made contact with nannies that the agencies thought would have a positive attitude towards nannying. However, the content of the interviews indicates otherwise: the nannies presented us with a very complex view of their work, highlighting both positive and negative aspects.

Regarding au pairs, we started out by trying to interview the few au pair agencies that exist in Sweden. However, several were reluctant to talk to us,[5] and as we soon found out that most au pair recruitments nowadays take place independently online,[6] we instead made use of a number of member-only au pair groups on Facebook. We got permission to place advertisements on these sites and were immediately contacted by several au pairs, who, in turn, also helped us get in contact with others interested in participating.

The Facebook groups turned out to be good sources for us to get a better understanding of the situation for au pairs in Sweden: the social interactions and activities they engaged in; what kinds of problems they face; and their occasional joint actions to try to solve these problems. In the threads, au pairs made contact with each other and arranged social events, as well as discussed wages, work permits, payment (or lack of payment) and how to get a social security number, and, occasionally, they also warned each other about problematic employers (see also Dalgas, 2015, 2016). The Facebook groups also turned out to be very important for parents in search of a new au pair, and for au pairs in search of host families.

While the recruitment of au pairs turned out to be relatively easy, we were unsuccessful in one respect: we did not get to meet with the ones in the most precarious positions. Through the narratives of the au pairs we met, rumours told to us by both au pairs and parents, and some posts on Facebook, we know that there is a group of au pairs who, for example, work without visas and who endure very tough working conditions (including sexual harassment) (see also Gavanas, 2013).[7]

Getting in contact with parents turned out to be more difficult, and we ended up using different channels. Some were accessed through nannies and au pairs: at the end of the interview, we (carefully) asked the nanny/au pair if she would be interested in putting us in contact with her employers. While some had no problem doing so, others declined.

We also accessed parents through snowballing on behalf of participating parents, as well as through posts in Facebook groups for au pairs.[8]

The children were contacted through their parents and were, in most cases, positive to participate: while initially being a bit shy, most children soon 'warmed up' and participated gladly in the drawing exercises that were presented to them. We paid close attention to their behaviour during the interviews: at any sign of them wanting to stop the interview, we interrupted the encounter (or started to do other things that the child wanted, like playing a game).

Participants

We met with and interviewed 73 actors involved in care practices in families that hire nannies and au pairs: 26 nannies and au pairs; 28 parents; and 19 children.[9]

Nannies and au pairs

We met with 11 nannies and 15 au pairs between the ages of 18 and 29 years, all of whom were women. This reflects the female dominance in the sector of childcare generally, and the domains of nanny and au pair care in particular.[10] The number of families that they had worked in varied. About half of the group had experience of working in only one family, while a couple had worked in as many as eight families. Taken together, they relate their experiences from working in 59 families.

The nannies were all employed through RUT agencies (see Chapter 1). All except three were born and raised in Sweden; three nannies came from Germany, Finland and Lithuania. All had been studying while taking on the job as nanny.[11] The Swedish-born nannies reported taking on the job to earn some extra money while studying, while, in contrast, the three nannies coming from abroad were more dependent on their nanny jobs to support themselves as they could not make use of the generous Swedish Study Loan system. A majority of the nannies came from a middle-class background, and, in many cases, their parents had university degrees.

Compared to the nannies, the au pairs represented a more diverse group. They came from different countries; seven were from within Europe (from Germany, Spain, the UK, Estonia and Lithuania) and eight were from outside the EU (from the Ukraine, Taiwan, the US, the Philippines and Macedonia).[12] Eleven of them had a university degree or had been studying at university level for some time before coming to Sweden.

The remainder had finished high school but had not been to university. Some sent remittances back home to their families. This was the case not only for au pairs from common sending countries such as the Philippines (which is a common practice identified by other Nordic researchers; Stenum, 2010; Bikova, 2017), but also for au pairs from parts of Europe where the financial crisis of the 1990s had hit hard.

Despite the prevalence of university education, one can still argue that the class position of nannies and au pairs is lower than that of the employing parents. In most cases, they came from an economically less privileged background, and, in addition, their position as nannies/au pairs put them in a relatively lower class position regardless of their habitus (Skeggs, 2004; Lawler, 2005).

Parents

We met and interviewed 28 parents in this research project – 19 mothers and nine fathers – all of whom lived in heterosexual couples. The parents decided for themselves whether they wanted to be interviewed together as a couple or separately; seven couple interviews were carried out within the project.

All participating parents were working full time in demanding careers and reported partners doing the same. Professions such as physician, lawyer, economist and chief executive officer (CEO) were common, and they often reported being in management positions. Their incomes (and sometimes assets) placed them in the upper-middle-class strata in Sweden (sometimes even higher). Eighteen of the 21 families in which we interviewed parents lived in or nearby metropolitan areas, which reflects the fact that RUT agencies are primarily established in these areas and that the practice of hiring au pairs seems to be more common in bigger cities.

The parents we interviewed (see Figure 1) had children between the ages of six months and 14 years, and the number of children in each family varied between one and four. Together, the families had experience of hiring 83 nannies and au pairs over the years, all women. All families had their children in public daycare (if the children were over the age of one year and under the age of six, which is the age for starting school in Sweden) concurrently with hiring nannies and au pairs. Several families had employed both nannies and au pairs, and a recurring pattern was that the families had started off hiring nannies by the hour, and then realised that they needed more – and more flexible – help. In some cases, the costs of hiring nannies by the hour got too high, and they therefore started to look for, and eventually hired, au pairs instead.

Figure 1: Participating parents and their children, nannies and au pairs

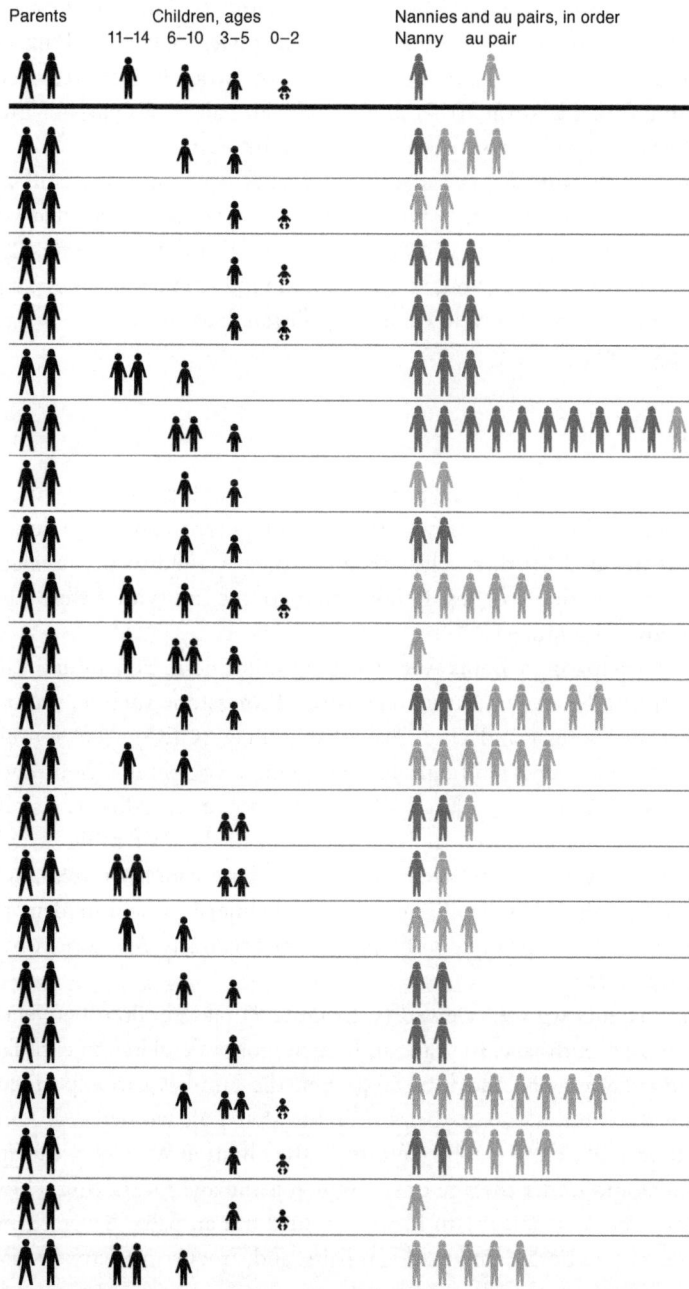

This figure shows the families of the participating parents, and the nannies and au pairs they have employed over the years. Note that not all parents have been interviewed in this study; in some cases only the father or the mother is participating. Neither all children nor all nannies and au pairs listed have participated.

Children

Nineteen children (nine girls and ten boys) aged between five and 14 years old with experience of being taken care of by nannies and au pairs were interviewed in this study. Most children were currently being taken care of by nannies or au pairs, while a few had no domestic caregivers at the moment, but had recent experiences to tell about. Some had had nannies or au pairs for as long as they could remember, some could not remember the names of them all and some children remembered as many as 11 nannies or au pairs, while others had just had one. Altogether, they related experiences of around 80 nannies and au pairs. Five children had had both nannies and au pairs, while two had only had nannies and 12 had only had au pairs.

Common to all children in this study is that both their parents were working full time (or more). Seventeen of the children lived together with their birth mother and birth father, and two had separated parents and lived part time with their mother and part time with their father, with the nanny or the au pair only present in one of the parent's households. The few children participating who were under the age of six attended daycare, the rest were in school during the days, and some children between the ages of six and ten years attended after-school care. Most were involved in many leisure-time activities in the afternoon, such as sports, music and other cultural activities.

Methods

We have made use of different methodological tools, suited for the particular actor and her/his position within the practice of everyday care, and focused on capturing the complex, multifaceted and often messy and shifting narratives of practices and relationships of care (see, for example, Mason, 2006; Smart, 2009; Gabb, 2010).

Nannies' and au pairs' interviews and diaries

The main focus in the interviews with nannies and au pairs was everyday care practice. We asked them to describe their day, and we encouraged them to talk about everyday incidents and things that they remembered about being in the family. We also asked them to tell us about and reflect upon their relationships with the different actors. Although we had an interview guide, this was adhered to rather loosely, and we instead tried to get the interviewees to speak freely and focus on what they themselves found important.

To encourage the nannies and au pairs to tell us about everyday events, we asked them to write a diary (Zimmerman and Wieder, 1977; Bolger et al, 2003). The instruction was to write some notes on what happened each day for one week. The participant was free to write about whatever she wanted, but we provided some optional questions to follow (a method comparable to memory books, see Thomson and Holland, 2005). Thirteen nannies and au pairs kept diaries; seven did the diary before the first interview and six did it afterwards. This meant that we had the possibility of meeting up with three nannies and three au pairs again for a second interview. These interviews were particularly fruitful as they gave us a much deeper and more complex understanding of the care work that they do and the relationships that they are involved in.[13]

Interviews with parents

The interviews with parents focused on the work and care situation in the family, and their experiences of employing nannies and au pairs. As in the interviews with nannies and au pairs, we also encouraged parents to talk about everyday doings, both describing a 'day' from morning to evening, and relating specific events that came to mind. In addition, we asked them to reflect upon both their own relationships to nannies and au pairs, and the relationships between nannies, au pairs and their children.[14]

Out of the total of 21 interviews, seven were couple interviews. These kinds of interviews offer other possibilities, including an analysis of interactions between the parties in the couple (Bjørnholt and Farstad, 2014). However, although some of the quotes in the chapter on parenting present couple interactions, we have chosen not to analyse these specifically in this book.

Drawing methods with children

In the encounters with the participating children, we offered the child the possibility to engage in drawing activities. First, a 'draw-your-day' exercise was introduced (Eldén, 2013a). This tool presents the child with a large piece of paper divided into four squares, and the instruction to 'draw your day' (drawing morning, lunchtime, afternoon and evening). During the drawing exercise, the child is asked by the researcher about the situation or object drawn, for example, 'Who's there with you?', 'Who is taking care of you?' and 'What are you/the others doing?'. Second, the tool of concentric circles of closeness was introduced (Smart et al, 2001; Mason and Tipper, 2008): the child was asked to draw him/herself in the inner circle and then to draw people 'who take care of you', 'who you take care of' and 'who are important to you' in the surrounding circles, with those most important/'those who take care of you most' placed closest to the child and those less important in the outer circles. These methods combined help the child to reflect upon and talk about the complexities of care: care as simultaneously practical doings, emotional doings and relationships. While the concentric circles zoom in more on relationships, the draw-your-day exercise takes doings and places as its point of departure.

While most children were happy to engage in the drawing exercises, some of the older children chose not to. In those cases, a more traditional interview was carried out but the focus here was also on the everyday, asking the child to describe his/her day and the carers involved in everyday situations, and to talk about their own relationships with nannies and au pairs.

Analysing the data

The analysis of these data was a constantly ongoing process with no definite beginning. As both researchers were involved in all parts of the research process, the continuous talks we had with each other, about observations on Facebook groups, impressions in interview encounters, readings and interpretations of transcribed interviews and literature, were the core of our joint analysis. This talk has kept the data alive and prevented the participants in the study from becoming flat examples on paper. These kinds of interactions are rarely mentioned in reports on analytical work as they are often difficult to pin down. However, and in line with the analytic contribution that we want to make in this book about the invisibility of care work, this invisible 'analysis work' is absolutely crucial for good qualitative analysis to happen.

We used different analytical tools to help us through all stages of the research process. After each interview, we took extensive field notes in which we reflected upon the interview as such, the interview situation and the feelings that the interview evoked for us, and seemed to evoke for the interviewee. These proved to be very useful in later stages of analysing and writing as accounts that quickly brought us back to the scene (Brannen, 2015).

All interviews were transcribed verbatim.[15] Thereafter, we read and reread them several times, and subsequently identified central themes in and across the data. Inspired by DeVault (1991), we especially looked for accounts about experiences that were hard to articulate. Care doings are often invisible even to the ones doing them; they are activities for which we lack an adequate language (DeVault, 1991: 228). To get at these doings, we looked specifically for discrepancies between accounts about how things 'should be' and accounts about actual events and practices. We were also attentive to moments of hesitation, contradiction and uses of expressions diminishing or explaining away experiences (Macdonald, 2010: 212).

Ethics when doing research in families

Doing research in families is a delicate matter, particularly so when several of the actors involved are in a vulnerable and subordinate position. As Jaqui Gabb (2010: 462) has argued, qualitative research that includes 'multiple accounts of self and different perspectives on shared relationships' requires careful ethical consideration all throughout the research process. However, if this is done, a mixed-methods approach including different actors' narratives about the same practice and relationships can yield rich and complex data for analysis, as we hope to show throughout this book.

Since the project includes children, it has, according to Swedish law, been tried in the Ethics Review Board.[16] However, the ethical questions were not solved by this approval; on the contrary, new ethical questions have emerged and been an integrated part of the whole research process.

This project can be said to entail elements of both studying 'up' and studying 'down' (Nader, 1979). We have studied young women in often precarious positions; children, who are in subordinate positions in relation to the adults in their surrounding everyday world; and also parents, who, in turn, have more power and resources compared to the others involved. To minimise the risk of putting nannies and au pairs in problematic positions, we did several things. First, we interviewed nannies and au pairs first and gave them the choice of allowing or refusing us access to their parent employers.[17] Second, in the cases where several adult members of the same family practice were interviewed, the nanny or the au pair was always interviewed by one of the researchers, and the parents by the other. This was done to ensure that no information on what the nanny or au pair had said would be passed on to the parents. The children were interviewed in the last stage, ensuring that no information from their interviews was accidently passed on to adult participants.[18]

After the completion of the interviews, we found ourselves in the delicate situation of having been trusted with personal narratives about the same practices and relationships, where the perspectives of the actors involved sometimes correlated well and sometimes diverged. The necessity of maintaining the anonymity between actors when writing about the data was obvious but tricky. When doing family case studies, it is very tempting to directly put together individual narratives, and compare and contrast them. While this was, indeed, done in our internal process of analysis, to report in this way is not ethical. Therefore, in writing about the data, we do not make explicit connections between participants in the study. In some cases, we write about and provide information from interviews done with actors involved in the same practice, but we never state who is connected to whom within the study. This is also the reason why we do not provide a list of participants in the study: by not connecting multiple characteristics to a specific actor, we are minimising the risk of identification. As is common in qualitative research, we have also changed names, locations and other circumstances, and have only included personal information about informants if it is important to the analysis.

Parents Employing Nannies and Au Pairs

Filippa

Filippa comes rushing into the coffee shop where we have agreed to meet for the interview. She is straight out of a meeting, and she immediately starts talking about her work as a chief executive officer for a large agency and her special interest in helping women in business pursue a career. "I'm a feminist careerist",[1] Filippa says. This also reflects back on Filippa's own everyday life. Gender equality is very important to Filippa, a mother of four children between the ages of five and ten years. However, while her husband has always supported her choices to pursue a demanding career, he has completely failed to do his part of the care and housework at home, she says. To solve the 'jigsaw puzzle of life', that is, to make the everyday life of managing a home, a family and a job possible, Filippa has hired help. Since their second child was born, Filippa has employed almost ten nannies, and she has recently also started to employ au pairs. This has been an absolute necessity, she says: "My husband works, and if I'm away, I have to cover for my absence somehow. He has said that explicitly, that he can only consider picking up the children from school and daycare once a week. There is no room for more in his schedule".

Hiring nannies and au pairs has not only been a way for Filippa to get through the everyday, it also has symbolic significance. She compares herself with her male colleagues who are married to women who work part time, or even, in a few cases, to housewives. "I also want a wife", she says jokingly, and then adds on a more serious note: "I want to show my daughters, I want to show my son too, that a mother isn't just someone who serves others, who stays at home". For Filippa, being a good parent is being present and engaged, and she sees herself as someone who always puts her children first. However, that does not necessarily mean that she always needs to be present *in person*. To be a good parent, you need to make sure that you are content and satisfied with your own life, she says, and that could sometimes mean *not* doing everything together with your children. For example, Filippa really dislikes taking her children to after-school activities: she cannot understand parents who follow their children to all these soccer practices and dance classes – "It's soo boring" – she says emphatically, and, she adds, probably not good for the children, either, since it turns them into "attention junkies". So, Filippa has delegated this to the nannies and au pairs that the family has hired.

The nannies, who have all been employed through RUT agencies, and by the hour, have mostly worked in the afternoons and early evenings: picking up the children from school and daycare; taking them to their many leisure-time activities; and, when coming back home again, making dinner for the whole family. For the au pairs, the added task has been helping out in the morning and also doing some lighter cleaning. This has enabled Filippa and her husband to work more hours, and also, on some occasions, to have some "me time", for going to the gym or meeting up with friends.

Some of the girls who have worked in the family have been wonderful, Filippa says. A few became really close to the children and felt like 'part of the family'. Filippa has never felt threatened by the close relationships that these nannies have formed with the children. On the contrary, she feels very secure in her own relationship to her children, so the fact that the children are loved by the nannies only means "more love" for her children, "more people who like them, and who they can love back", and "more people to confide in".

However, although Filippa has a positive attitude towards hiring nannies and au pairs, she has had some bad experiences as well. Filippa tells us about one occasion when the family had two nannies employed at the same time since their demands for help were great. The nannies were dissatisfied with the family's unpredictable schedules. The initially agreed-upon schedule of spending some hours with the children in the afternoon might seem simple and clear-cut, but Filippa stresses how important it is that the nannies are flexible and able to adjust to the family's needs. With her and her husband's working situation, it is impossible to plan ahead, she says. Some weeks they needed help every day, some weeks they needed less. The nannies started to ask for regular schedules, which made Filippa annoyed. She started to look for au pairs instead; in Filippa's mind, an au pair is more present, and she felt that this would more easily meet the family's needs for 'flexibility'.

Filippa's narrative shares similarities with many of the narratives that we listened to in our interviews with Swedish parents hiring nannies and au pairs. It illuminates how doing family with the help of nannies and au pairs draws on strong discourses of family and care in Sweden, such as the almost ever-present discourses of gender equality in both women's and men's accounts of their family life, as well as concerns with 'solving the jigsaw puzzle of life' (Roman and Peterson, 2011). It further necessitates a questioning and reformulation of parenting ideals, where the idea of 'quality time' is significant, and it also means reflecting on one's own relationship to one's child in a new way, as well as the relationship between the child and the nanny/au pair: sometimes, a nanny or an au pair becomes 'close', almost like 'part of the family', but at other times, she is more like an 'employee' carrying out a service. Most importantly, Filippa's and the other parents' narratives about how they have ideally pictured the involvement of nannies and au pairs and the care work that they should be carrying out in the family do not correspond completely with the actual experiences of the practice: nanny and au pair care often turns out to be a rather complex matter.

Employer parents in Sweden

The context for doing parenting in Sweden has changed over the last decades. As we argued in Chapter 1, new ideals can be detected, visible both in politics and policies. While the welfare institutions of public daycare and extensive and shared parental leave, coming out of and realising ideals of social equality and gender equality, are still standing strong, they are complemented by new ideals of privatisation, parents' 'right to choose' and intensive parenting (Sparrman et al, 2016). When the right-wing government introduced the RUT tax deduction and thereby encouraged extensive growth in a previously marginal domestic service market, the 'right to choose' ideal was merged with (at least part of) the gender-equality ideal: parents should have the opportunity to choose to get help in carrying out everyday caring chores at home (cleaning and nanny care) so that women would have the opportunity to pursue careers on more equal terms to men.

However, not all Swedish families have the financial opportunity to make use of the RUT deduction or hire au pairs. The majority of the tax deductions are made by families with high economic standards, and this is, indeed, visible in the group of parents participating in our study.

As presented in Chapter 2, all of the 28 parents interviewed in this study live in couples of dual earners, often with demanding careers and with good (sometimes very good) financial means. This was reflected in the environments that we, as researchers, met when we entered the homes of these families. Several lived in big houses or apartments in affluent areas. While most of them showed signs of common elements of 'family living', with children's toys spread out on the floor, or dirty raincoats and wellingtons in the hallway, signs of affluence were also often visible: newly renovated kitchens; several and quite expensive cars in the driveway; and occasionally swimming pools or private access to the beach. However, we have also met with parents who live quite average middle-class lives, families that neither are wealthy nor have to worry particularly about making ends meet. While parents in the former category more often report a presence of nannies and au pairs even before the introduction of the RUT deduction, for parents in the latter category, the tax deduction seems to have played a role in the decision to hire help. Some parents talked about being reluctant to tell others about their having nannies and au pairs, expecting negative comments about not being able to care for their own children or 'showing off' their wealth (see also Aarseth, 2014), but several parents found themselves in social contexts (and residential areas) where 'everyone' employed nannies, au pairs and other domestic workers. Many also talked appreciatively about the fact that attitudes are changing: more and more families are starting to hire nannies and au pairs (as well as other domestic services), and it is becoming more and more accepted in society as a legitimate solution to the 'jigsaw puzzle of life'.

So, what does it entail, then? What are the contours of this new doing of care and family in the Swedish families who have the financial wherewithal and have chosen to hire nannies and au pairs? In this chapter, we will first look at what the parents think they 'gain' from hiring nannies and au pairs, a discussion that centres on new ways of doing gender equality, 'good parenting' and 'solving the jigsaw puzzle of life'. Second, we turn to the parents' ideas on what kind of 'care doing' they expect the nanny to perform in the family. What parts of care is she supposed to do, according to the parents, and what is 'good nanny care'? This leads us into our next and third focus: the ways in which the parents look upon the relationship between the nanny/au pair and their children, and the question of the inevitable break-ups when nannies and au pairs leave a family. Finally, we zoom in on ideas about what the nanny's role is in the family, centred on the distinctions between being 'part of the family' or 'just an employee'.

Solving the 'jigsaw puzzle of life'

The parents in our study recurrently refer to their hiring of nannies and au pairs as a 'buying of time'. Buying time means buying the time of others, of domestic workers who do things that the parents themselves would have done otherwise, but it also means paying for the possibility of filling your time with other activities. Concern with time – controlling, managing, protecting and, not least, creating 'family time' – is, as Daly (1996) has argued, a central practice that families engage in (see also Näre and Wide, forthcoming). However, it is also a concern whose content and contours shift depending on historical and social context. The social position of the family – and of actors within the family – affects the ways in which time in families can be controlled and delineated, and thereby affects the family practices that come to constitute the family. In the following, we will look at what the parents hiring nannies and au pairs 'gain' through this arrangement: what comes out of this buying of time?

Gender equality, good couples and different femininities

One of the main arguments put forward by the proponents of the RUT deduction reform was about gender equality: the 'failed' gender equality of Swedish dual-earner couples was to be solved by the creation of a market for domestic services. This argument is, indeed, a recurrent one among the parents that we interviewed: having nannies and au pairs makes possible the realisation of gender equality within the couple. Paula, for example, a mother of three small children, who has hired several nannies over the years, sees RUT as the reason that she and her husband have been able to live in a "balanced" and "very gender-equal" relationship: "RUT has facilitated a lot, that is, for women, to be able to work more without having this constant bad conscience about the home", she says.

A crucial component in the 'buying of time' is buying time for the mother (in the heterosexual family) to pursue a career that is as demanding as her husband's without having to feel bad about neglecting her responsibilities at home. This attests to the fact that there are still strong expectations of women to be the primarily responsible party for care work at home, something that the participants in our study – both men and women – are quite aware of. Leif, for example, a father of three middle-school-aged children who have been taken care of by many au pairs during their childhood, tells us about the negotiations that he and his wife had when the children were small: who was to stay home and sacrifice his or her career? Both he and his wife had completed similar university education, and neither of them wanted to reduce their hours. Also, he says, the expectations of them as mother and father were different: it is the woman who is expected to sacrifice her career. Leif is very aware that the au pairs have relieved him of having to take on a greater responsibility at home, a responsibility that you might expect of "modern couples", he says: "If you have an au pair, you don't need to choose". Similarly, Gunnar, the father of two children, admits that the au pairs that the family has hired have enabled him to take a step back from caring responsibilities:

> 'I would say that we have become, somehow, I think we have almost become less gender equal. [...][2] I have always cooked too little food at home, but now I hardly ever cook. If you look at the practical things we do in the house, then I think …
> I do think we are very gender equal when it comes to who decides what and those kinds of things, then we are very gender equal…. But, otherwise, I think I've become more of an old fart since we got an au pair, really … if I'm allowed to be a bit self-critical.'

Gunnar has been able to take on a more traditionally male role in the family since they started to hire au pairs; the few things related to care work that he previously did are now no longer necessary, he argues. Similarly, Emma, the mother of three children, talks about her hiring of nannies as a "buying of time" both for herself, so that she can pursue a career, and for her husband. He could have spent the one day a week when he is not at work doing chores at home, she says, but through the buying of domestic services, he does not have to:

> 'We buy the services he would have been doing if we were in a more gender-equal relationship. It's like if you look at it, look at how it should be in a modern relationship with two academics who both think it is challenging to have a career …
> I wouldn't have, if we hadn't had these services, I would have had to force him to come home, and that would have been difficult. [...] So, for me, this has been a way of not having to … not taking on … that fight, which, if I had forced him to be at home, because I could have done that too – but that would have come with a huge cost for our relationship.'

The costs that Emma refers to are the conflicts that she can now avoid, both the fights over whose career is to be sacrificed when the children arrive, and the everyday fights over housework. Several mothers and fathers bring this to our attention: the buying of services enhances the quality of the couple relationship through the reduction of conflicts. In fact, fights over care and housework have been identified in previous research as a primary case for conflict and divorce in Swedish couples, explained as a consequence of the strong official gender-equality discourse that fuels these conflicts when couples fail to live up to the ideal (Nordenmark, 2008). Based on the 'right' she has with reference to gender equality, Emma feels that, on the one hand, she could demand that her husband takes on a greater responsibility at home but, on the other, she knows that this would make her the one who crushes his dreams. She does not want to be the "brake pad" for his ambitions, she says. Buying help is an easier solution that does not jeopardise the relationship between the two of them.

Within the ideal of gender equality also lies the possibility of women performing a different kind of femininity, diverging from traditional norms. In the introductory example, Filippa was an example of this. Pursuing a career on the same terms as her husband becomes a way of challenging dominant motherhood ideals for Filippa, of distancing herself from a stereotypical feminine model of caring, "of serving others", as she puts it. Ann-Katrin, the mother of two children, similarly talks about and contrasts herself to the wives of her male colleagues, women, "working part time in, like, daycare or preschools". Being a career mother is defined in opposition to other women: those women who choose less demanding and more traditional, caring jobs, and who then also do more care work at home. That is not the kind of femininity or motherhood ideal that these women value for themselves or want to pass on to their children.

The gender-equal couple that is made possible through the hiring of nannies and au pairs (and other kinds of domestic help) diverges from the previously dominant ideal of gender equality in Sweden as a sharing of not only earner responsibilities, but also caring responsibilities. It enables men to again take a step back and refrain from doing care work while not hindering women from obtaining demanding careers. Gender equality is reformulated into the equal opportunity of both parties to pursue a career, without having to sacrifice one's time and energy on domestic work at home. 'Buying time' becomes a way of buying the possibility of women to pursue 'non-traditional' femininities, as well as the possibility of having a more conflict-free couple relationship, and also, as we shall see in the following, reducing conflicts in relation to children.

The stress-free family, quality time and care without conflicts

A subject brought up by all parents interviewed in this study is that the 'buying of time' through employing nannies and au pairs is a way of solving the 'jigsaw puzzle of life', that is, to make the everyday life of managing a home, family and job possible. Descriptions of the work–family dilemma occur in the parents' narratives when talking about the time before (or being 'in between') the hiring of nannies and au pairs. Work demands emerge as a constant in most of the parents' narratives: work is described as demanding full attention, flexibility and readiness to step in whenever there is a need, and there is hardly anything one can do to change that. As Emma says, discussing her work situation, if you are working part time, you "do not get the good assignments", but rather "send out a clear signal to your employer that you are not prioritising work". Demands from home, or, rather, demands to be a 'good parent', are also felt strongly, especially by women. As we have seen, both men and women talk about the greater pressure on women of doing the caring part, coming through in different settings. The expectation to pick children up early from daycare is a recurrent theme in the interviews, and, indeed, one that has also been identified in other research (Lorentzi, 2011; Alsarve et al, 2017). As argued in Chapter 1, public daycare centres are used extensively by Swedish parents and are highly valued and trusted. However, in recent years, there has been a debate on how many hours a child should spend in daycare (partly fuelled by cutbacks made in the sector), and discourses of the harm of having children at daycare for too many hours are spreading (Lorentzi, 2011). For the parents in our study, limiting the time the children spend in daycare is a primary concern and a motivation for hiring a nanny or an au pair. The time she spends with the children is portrayed as qualitatively different from the child's time in daycare, and contrasts are drawn between the 'stressful' environment of public daycare, on the one hand, and the possibility of having the full attention of one adult – the nanny or the au pair – in the calm atmosphere of the home, on the other.

A narrative shared by all of the parents in our study is that of the reduction of stress in everyday life that has occurred when a nanny or an au pair has entered the family. The reduction of stress is felt by the parents, who do not have to include their children in morning or afternoon scheduling, an arrangement that is assumed to be good for all, parents and children alike. Ingvar, for example, the father of four children, talks about the hiring of au pairs as a way of "taking stress out of the everyday life of the children". Ingvar paints a vivid picture of their otherwise hectic schedule: of children needing to be taken to school and activities; of dinner that has to be bought, cooked and put on the table; in the midst of immense work demands. It is "this puzzle" he says, and the au pair makes all the difference:

> 'It is those two hours in the morning and the two hours later on. When we get home, like a normal time, five, maybe, then the table is set already, or sometimes we start cooking right away, and then someone has already gotten milk at the store; there is fruit, there is food. The children have been picked up from school, and they have already been to their activities.'

The critical moments identified by Ingvar of getting ready to leave for work and school, and of returning home in the afternoon, are mentioned by many parents, and these are the times when the help of nannies and au pairs is most wanted. For example, Tomas, the father of two small children, talks about the "witching hour between half past four and half past five":

> 'when the children are hungry and you yourself are hungry too, and you should be cooking dinner and you've stressed like a maniac out of a meeting to get in time to daycare to pick up the children and then hurry home to make food and then you have another meeting with those American clients at eight o'clock at night, and so on and so forth.'

To do this without the help of an au pair would not make Tomas "as harmonious as I would like to be with the children", which would affect the children negatively. In Chapter 4, we will return to the descriptions of this "witching hour", there described in the narratives of nannies and au pairs, and we will see that the 'reduction of stress' argument is more complex than the parents might think: in many ways, the stress and the hardship are still very much present, but they are now experienced by the nannies and au pairs instead of the parents.

Hiring someone else to do parts of care can also make the caring chores that one actually performs into a more positive experience. Knowing that there are no household chores to attend to, for example, after putting the children to bed at night, makes the 'tucking in' a much more enjoyable experience. Ingrid, the mother of four children, talks about the enhancement in the care chores she does that can happen when someone else takes care of the mundane everyday doings. Giving the children a bath becomes a more fun activity when it is not a necessity, she says:

'You ask the au pair, "Could you please give the children a bath?" – otherwise, it turns into an obligation for us. Then we can do it in a relaxed and enjoyable way at the weekend, instead. Not that we miss out on it; rather, you share it a little more. It becomes a better experience for the children and they get, like, time to play in the tub for half an hour if they want, instead of us saying that they should have a bath in five minutes.'

For Ingrid, the doing of caring chores, such as giving a child a bath, is not *in itself* problematic or even boring as long as it is not in the context of being a necessity and part of the everyday routine. Vera, a mother of three, and with experience of hiring many au pairs, talks in similar terms about the importance for her and her husband of not being exposed to everyday caring necessities:

'She [the au pair] has unburdened us so, so much. That she, she takes on, like, the whole buffer time, she takes upon herself this time, like we have never really had to go to the supermarket with our children screaming on the floor, pulling our legs. You never have to experience that, really, like, being really exhausted, since she [the au pair] also makes dinner for all of us, so neither I nor my husband have ever had to stand there by the stove preparing meatballs and pasta with all the children screaming around you. And, I have to say, we're really bad at those everyday situations, to handle those, we have kind of realised that. [...] We have realised that that's our limit for what we can handle as a family and in our relationship, so we better try to avoid these situations, and the few times it happens nowadays, then it is just a one-time incident; it is not this everyday thing that happens regularly. Because it is the everyday stuff, the things that recur, we cannot handle that.'

The everyday caring necessities are not for Vera and her husband. They have tried this once many years ago, she tells us, and it almost led to a break-up of the marriage. This construction of certain care doings as 'not suited for me' is an argument found in other research on people buying domestic services (see, for example, Anderson, 2000; Holmqvist, 2015). It builds on the assumption that it is possible to divide care into 'spiritual' and 'menial' doings (Roberts, 1997), and points especially towards the role of mundanity: it is not necessarily the content of the chore *as such* that determines whether the parent wants to carry it out or not; rather, it is the possibility of doing it at the time one chooses, not all the times that it is necessary (Christensen, 2002: 79). In this way, the parents' economic possibility of 'buying time' (Daly, 1996: 108) gives them control of the care situation and enables them to realise an everyday family life – in their view – of reduced stress. The conviction that everyday family life without stress is possible without compromising ambitions at work, or defaulting to gender inequality, runs through all interviews with the parents in this study. The solution is to hire nannies and au pairs: to have them be the "extra wife" that Filippa called for in the introductory example. This not only enables the parents – and, most importantly, the mothers – to have a demanding career, but also enables *better* parenting: being more 'present in the moment' when they spend time with their children since they do not have to do all the everyday mundane caring necessities. Thus, the time spent with the children becomes *quality time* for all.

Dividing care: what nannies and au pairs (should) do

The possibilities of doing a modified form of gender equality, with a focus on the right of both parents to have a career, entails a distancing on the part of some women from 'traditional' ideals of caring motherhood and femininity. At the same time, the solution that they are suggesting reaffirms those same ideals: the care work that they refrain from (or could not get their husbands to do) is still to be performed by women, but by 'other' women. In this section, we turn to the actual content of the nannies' and au pairs' doings, as they are perceived and talked about by the parents.

Underlying the whole idea of hiring a nanny or an au pair is the possibility of delegating care: she is assumed to be able to step in and do some of the work that needs to be done around children, while other tasks and dimensions may be kept by the parents. When the parents talk about some parts of care – at certain moments and under certain conditions – as being 'for them', as we saw in the previous section, while other parts can more easily (and better) be carried out by their nannies and au pairs, the idea of care as consisting of 'menial' and 'spiritual' parts is reproduced (Roberts, 1997). However, looking more closely at parents' expectations and descriptions of *the actual doing* of nannies and au pairs in everyday life, as well as their descriptions of what characterises a 'good' nanny or au pair, delegating turns out to be rather complex.

Tensions in expectations: hours, lists and independence in the 'easy job' of a 'family project leader'

A recurrent concern in talking about the doings of the nannies and au pairs in the family is hours: what is she expected to do during the hours that she is 'on duty', what chores can she be expected to manage? Talk about hours is, indeed, more present in interviews with parents who hire au pairs than with parents employing nannies. While the number of hours, at least ideally, is more set when it comes to nannies (who are paid by the hour for the time they spend in the family), the rules for au pairs are less clear. All parents interpret the au pair rule of 25 hours of 'light housework' per week differently, and as studies have shown, the fact that the au pair is almost always living under the same roof as the family makes it difficult to draw the line between work and leisure (Anderson, 2000; Cox, 2006, 2015; Búriková and Miller, 2010).

Nelly (mother of four children), for example, is well aware of the 25-hour rule for au pairs, and of the fact that the family sometimes breaks this rule. It might be that our au pair works a bit more, Nelly admits, "especially when the children are ill" and she takes care of them the whole day. This is a very common use of au pairs among the parents in our study: to have the au pairs care for the children when they are ill so that the parents do not need to stay home from work. While some compensate for this by paying extra, most parents see it as a taken-for-granted part of the au pair's work and do not count the extra hours, often downplaying the work by saying things like "the children are not sick that often anyway", or, as with Nelly, saying that it is probably evened out in the end since the au pair might get extra days off some time, so "it is not a problem". In fact, all through her description of the au pair's work day, Nelly continually uses the expression of "it is not a problem", and also stresses the great flexibility of the au pair to "choose for herself" when during the day she attends to the different chores that the parents have asked her to do. A regular day for Nelly's au pair starts at 7.15 am, when she helps the children get ready to go to daycare and school, after which she takes them to daycare around 8.30 am:

'After that, she has *her time off* until three, or half-past four in the afternoon. So, during the day, *she can choose for herself* if she wants to take the dogs out for a walk before or after the children get home. It doesn't matter, but, of course, it is better [if she walks them during the day]. But she loves to take the dogs out for a walk, so *it is not a problem* for her. But *she can choose for herself* if she wants to do it after three o'clock with the children, or before. [...] And then she picks up the children at daycare, and it depends, sometimes there are swimming lessons, or they have sports or dancing lessons, so then it is driving them there ... and then making dinner [...] and then ... vacuum clean if that is needed, and *she can choose when she wants to do that*, during the day or, like, between four and six in the afternoon; it doesn't matter. And laundry, or not do laundry, but like fold everything and iron, it becomes quite a lot when you have four children [laughs]. [...] So, maybe, that isn't something that the au pairs particularly like, but [laughs].... Sometimes, she says, "Yes, but I watch TV while doing it", so ... *it could maybe be nice*. [...] That is a couple of hours a week maybe [laughs]. But *she can do it when they [the children] are home*, so it is included in her hours. And then after dinner, I have been away all day, so I like to spend time with the children, really, to take care of them, give them a bath, so most of the time, the au pair, yes, actually, she did that from the start, she said, "No, I'll take care of the kitchen", so she puts everything in the dishwasher and cleans up everything there, and then she comes upstairs and helps out with brushing their teeth and getting them into their pyjamas and all. And, sometimes, she reads them a story, depending on whether I want to go exercising in the evening.' (Emphases added)

Nelly also mentions later on that the au pair sometimes shops for food and that she is responsible for cooking dinner for the whole family on all weeknights. She also babysits some evenings, either on weekdays or on the weekends when the parents are away. When recalling the everyday chores in the interview, Nelly herself seems to become aware of the fact that the family is exceeding the work hours for the au pair: obviously so when the au pair cares for a sick child, but the au pair also exceeds the 25-hour limit during a regular week. Framing the au pair's hours alone during the day as a time when she is "off", despite the fact that she is expected to do several things, works in her narration by her stressing that the au pair could *choose* to do all these things when the children are home (something that according to the au pair and nanny narratives presented in Chapter 4 is very difficult indeed). By assuring the interviewer that "it is not a problem", and saying (by quoting the au pair from memory) that the au pair really does not mind doing all this work and that she actually suggested some of it herself, the au pair's quite vast hours and responsibilities are framed as easy and free.

While labelling the work they delegate to nannies and au pairs as easy, free and independent, most parents also detail in written lists or verbal instructions what they expect her to do. Samuel and Stina, the parents of four children, are more careful than Nelly in counting the hours in order to not exceed the 25-hour limit: "We have calculated that it takes about two hours a day to do household chores, like laundry and cleaning the house", but, as they say, "it is all up to the au pair when she chooses to do them". This makes them characterise the au pair's work as "a job with lots of freedom": "There are things we expect them to do but we stay out of how they do it, just so that it gets done", and "We have to assume that they are independent adults who can take on the responsibility of getting certain things done", Samuel says. They also show the researcher lists that they hand to the au pair, detailing her daily schedule, and special lists for the cleaning procedures, saying that "We have a very thorough review in the beginning of exactly what we expect from them when it comes to cleaning".

The detailing is, as we have seen, coupled with a stress on freedom and independence. Expectations that the nanny/au pair will 'take the initiative' are very much present in the parents' narratives. A good nanny or au pair is someone you can trust will get things done, even though you have not stated the chore explicitly. Ofelia (a mother of two), for example, compares the family's first au pair with the ones that they have had later on. The first one was not as good as the later ones as she was just doing the designated tasks: "She never did anything extra", "It was never like she realised herself that she should start the laundry", Ofelia says. Ofelia is reluctant to criticise her for this; after all, she is very careful not to be seen as someone who expects her au pair to do more than the agreed-upon hours and tasks. However, she *is* still expecting more. This becomes apparent when she describes other au pairs who had been working in the family, the last one of whom quit the family some months earlier, leaving them with no au pair:

> 'I felt like there was always a backup. I didn't need to leave work, like, at an exact time, I could come home late some days … and then all this […] project leading that you do all the time with all the packed lunches, all those outdoor days at school, all the gym clothes you have to remember.… And I got so much help with that, and now [that the au pair has quit] the children turn to me for this, and suddenly I feel … I know my husband doesn't think there is a difference since she quit, but I do. I feel like now I have to take care of all this by myself, and I feel so bad if I forget a packed lunch for an outdoor day, and I do that sometimes nowadays. Because she

always reminded me, she was, like, engaged in all this too, it was more like being relieved of the stress, of not always having to be the one at the steering wheel, and then like … with clothes and stuff for the children, she reminded me, like, "Doesn't he need a new pair of shoes now?". And it was just so nice to have someone who double-checked.'

Ofelia describes the good au pair as someone with whom she could share the responsibility of "project leading" the family as she relieved Ofelia of the responsibility of "always being the one at the steering wheel" since she saw the things that needed to be done. The engagement of a good nanny or au pair in the family is an engagement beyond the designated tasks. As Nelly says about her current au pair, "she is so kind", "helpful" and "independent": "She thinks about everything, she remembers everything I forget [laughs]. Like, 'Today, they have an outdoor day in school' or 'Today, it's swimming lessons' or … yes, they are taking dance classes, and then she has that under control too [laughs]. She is a real household manager".

While some parents worry about 'using' their nannies or au pairs too much, the counting of hours is most often thought of as going against the character of the 'free' and 'easy' characterisation of the job, as well as the 'always available and willing to step in' expectations of a good nanny or au pair. If the counting of hours is done by the nanny or the au pair, it is generally not appreciated. To avoid this, some parents who know that they often exceed the allowed hours take action: one mother talks about giving the au pair an extra €50 a month: "then I don't want any whining about the hours", "not that they should work themselves to death, but show some good will". Counting hours in these cases becomes detrimental to one of the primary reasons they have for hiring au pairs and nannies: that they should be *flexible* and *able to adjust* themselves to the family's changing needs. This wish for flexibility is stressed by many parents, including the ones providing lists and schedules. Ingvar and Ingrid, for example, show the researcher the detailed weakly schedule they give to their au pairs, but then still stress the importance of her being flexible. A good au pair, like the one they employ now, is "incredibly helpful", "very flexible" and prepared to step in whenever needed, in contrast to previous bad ones, who were "very rigid" and refused to work passed their hours. In some cases, the lack of flexibility has even led the parents to prematurely terminate agreements with au pairs and nannies.

On top of solving the jigsaw puzzle of life, some parents also expect nannies and au pairs to contribute with something *different* to the child's everyday life. Paula, for example, talks about the nanny as someone who "enriches" the child, someone with whom you do "different things" compared to what you do with your mother and father (see also Tronto, 2002). The 'different things' that are expected from nannies and au pairs often entail expectations on the part of the parents regarding what activities the nanny or au pair should do with the children, and ideas about her special qualities or knowledge that she is expected to pass on. Nelly, for example, expected their current au pair to teach her children to play the piano, and she is a bit disappointed, she tells us, that this did not happen. In general, parents often have ideas about what the nanny or au pair should do when she is together with the children, and screen time – using tablets, computers and TV – is generally discouraged, while crafting, singing, baking and being outdoors are portrayed as good activities (see also Dermott and Pomatti, 2015). Specific skills, such as speaking a different language, are most commonly asked for, and the au pair's ability to tutor the children in English is especially highly desired.

While some parents are very upfront with what qualitative activities and skills they expect from a nanny or an au pair, others are more reluctant and ambivalent in what they think they can expect. Darina (a mother of two), for example, stresses that her primary expectation of a nanny is for her to "be engaged with the children, not just stand there and watch them and just let them run". To give the children extra attention, to actively engage with them and to show them that she is there for them is what Darina expects, and if the nanny also wants to educate the children on top, it becomes a very positive added value, she says.

The enterprise of delegating care that parents take upon themselves when hiring a nanny or an au pair, in practice, entails several tensions and ambiguities. First, the idea that it is possible to estimate the time it takes to do care work is both embraced and disregarded by the parents. It is the parents who have the ultimate power to decide how much (and what kind of) care work should be expected of the nanny or the au pair during the hours that she is supposed to work, who sometimes explicitly, sometimes implicitly, estimate how many hours each chore should take, and who suggest different 'qualitative activities' that she should engage in. However, at the same time, the hardship and significance of the care work is downplayed in delineating the nanny/au pair job as easy, in talk about one's children as easy to work with, in suggestions of the possibility of doing multiple tasks (eg ironing while being with the children), and in assurances that the nanny/au pair 'does not mind' taking on more hours or doing extra work. The parents are in control and have the power to define and orchestrate the care situation that nannies and au pairs find themselves in, and in doing so, the parents rely heavily on the premise that it is possible to divide up care into manageable blocks of time (Tronto, 2002: 44). However, even when all the work that is detailed is, indeed, carried out by the nanny or the au pair, the parents still signal that this is not really enough after all. This points towards a second, and very important, tension in the parents' expectations and talk about nanny/au pair doings: a good nanny or au pair does something *beyond* the detailed lists (or verbal agreements) of chores. She is flexible and available to step in when needed, she 'remembers' and knows without having to be reminded, she 'sees' what needs to be done, she 'knows' and she 'takes initiative': she puts on the laundry when clothes are dirty, and she remembers and packs the children's backpacks on the outing days. She *engages* with the children. All this work cannot and is not detailed in lists; it is not explicitly delegated by the parents, but it is still expected of the nanny and the au pair. It is precisely the parts of care that Jennifer Mason (1996) labels sentient activity, the 'thinking' and 'knowing' activities that are necessary for a care situation to work. However, these expectations of care are difficult for the parents to nail down and talk about, as they also are for the nannies and au pairs themselves, as we shall see in Chapter 4.

Nannies, au pairs and children: closeness and (unproblematic) break-ups

The ambiguities in the expectations of the nanny's/au pair's care also appear in relation to parents' reflections on the relationships that are formed between her and the child. This becomes particularly visible in talk about entrances and exits of nannies and au pairs, and the parents' ideas about how this affects their children.

"More love for my children": positive closeness of nanny, au pair and child relations

Compared to parents in other studies of nanny and au pair care, the ones we interviewed are not very concerned with the fact that the nannies and the au pairs they hire form close relationships with their children (Macdonald, 2010). With a few exceptions,[3] the general attitude among the parents is relaxed in relation to questions of closeness. A good nanny/ au pair is expected to form close bonds with the children; in fact, if this does not happen, she is not good from the perspective of the parents. As expressed by Filippa, "[t]he more people who love them, who they can love back", the better.

A 'more love for my children' attitude is also visible in Kicki's (a mother of two children) description of the au pairs' relationships to her children.

Kicki herself does not really like her current au pair, "we don't click", as she says, but she is aware of the fact that her children do, and that the feelings between them and the au pair are mutual:

> 'I do see that our au pair really likes our children. She hugs them and … like, you can really see that, when you look at her, she kisses them and cuddles with them and tickles them, like physically. I see that she really, really likes our children. And laughs together with them and thinks they are funny, and still she dares to say "no", so you feel like there is something genuine there. She doesn't just do that because it's her job.'

The strong feelings between the children and the au pair are, however, not threatening to Kicki, not even given the fact that she herself does not really like the au pair. She is not worried that they will become too close, she says; rather, "It is good that they have confidence in her", but she adds that she does get a bit annoyed when the children call for the au pair when she herself is present. Ann-Katrin has experience of actions that she interprets as her children "punishing" her for being away and leaving them with the au pair (whom they really like), but this is not upsetting to Ann-Katrin. On the contrary, she sees it as something to be expected:

> 'My daughter said to me last spring that they could have a mummy robot, instead, since I was away so much [laughs], since I wasn't home. So, I think, for me, it's more, for me, it is a natural part of the fact that I chose not to be at home all the time, and then I feel that it is really very good that they feel so safe with her [the au pair]. […] It would have been horrible if they didn't feel safe with the person who picks them up and leaves them at school.'

To Ann-Katrin, the children's behaviour is to be expected. It is something to be counted on when you organise your life the way in which she does. The fact that the au pair spends substantial amounts of time with the child does make the forming of a close bond inevitable, she argues.

Part of life or heartbreaking: parents' views on break-ups

Most parents expect and want a close relationship to be developed between the nanny/au pair and their children, although they are aware that this does not always happen. There is also an awareness of the possibility of close relationships being formed even if the parent is not him/herself particularly interested in the au pair. However, what about the break-ups of these relationships? If the parents expect – and sometimes facilitate and encourage – the forming of close, specific bonds, how do they then look upon the breaking of these bonds?

In Sweden, nannies and au pairs are not commonly involved in families for longer periods of time. If official au pair rules are followed, an au pair is only hired for one year, and RUT nannies are intended to be a shorter engagement on the part of the nannies as they are often recruited for 'extra jobs' during their studies. Although the official rules and standards are not always followed, the families we met in this study all used short-term nannies and au pairs, with most having nannies and au pairs who have been employed around a year, and the maximum employment engagement of a couple of families being around three years. However, many have employed nannies and au pairs sequentially and thus have experience of hiring and saying goodbye to them, and then hiring new nannies and au pairs.

When we asked the parents about their experience of hiring and ending contracts with nannies and au pairs, we were told many stories about hiring processes – about getting better at selecting nannies and au pairs over the years, and of having learned to identify 'good girls' (mentioning characteristics such as being from the countryside and having younger siblings as good features, and Facebook pictures of partying as not so good), of Skype interviews or recorded videos with RUT nannies, of in-home visits where it is possible to watch the nanny interact with the children, and so forth. Several also brought up their worries about how they were going to deal with the 'jigsaw puzzle of life' when the nanny or au pair left, and many told us about outsourcing the recruitment of new nannies and au pairs to the 'old' one, and of having her train the new one by working side by side for a couple of days.

The subject of children's reactions to nannies and au pairs coming and leaving was less talked about, despite us asking explicitly about this. A reoccurring narrative portrayed the process of both getting to know and leaving as something that the children have learned to deal with over the years. Vera, for example, remembers that hiring the first au pair was not a problem at all, but that when they were to switch to a new one for the first time, it became difficult, although this also worked out eventually:

'Then the Filipino girl arrived and that was probably the hardest part, actually, because then they [the children] were big enough to be aware of a new person arriving […] but she did really well. She was amazing with the children, like, you

51

know, you just wonder, "God, do these kinds of people exist?".
So, she, I don't know what she did really, but after two days,
they just loved her! [...] And then, the next girl, she was from
Taiwan, and then the children had learned the system. They
were getting it, that we have someone here who helps out.'

The children "learned the system", Vera says; they learned that girls come
and go, and this made the transitions easy. The same goes for break-
ups; since the au pairs they have hired have all been good at staying in
contact, the break-ups have not felt that dramatic. It has been a "gradual
process" where the children become less and less interested in keeping in
contact, Vera says. Similarly, Ann-Katrin and Arvid, who have experience
of saying goodbye to several nannies and au pairs, see the sad part as an
inevitable consequence of the situation, but as something that passes. "We
all cry" when they leave, they say, and it is hard for the children: they
talk about their youngest child suddenly wanting them to buy an extra
cookie for an au pair, although she had left a long time ago. However,
over the years, the children have learned that the au pairs are "temporary
relationships", something that has also affected their way of connecting
with new au pairs: they "restrain themselves", Arvid says, and, in the end,
they learn that the one relationship that is lasting is that of the parents.
This also solves the question of becoming 'too close': as they grow older,
the children learn to self-regulate and never allow the nanny or the au pair
to get close in the first place, Arvid argues.

In general, the parents talk very little about how nannies and au pairs
react to break-ups. Samuel and Stina are among the few who do, and in
their experience, the break-up is, indeed, harder for the au pairs than for
their children. The children have no problem adapting to new au pairs,
they say, "They change au pairs as easy as they change socks", but it seems
to be more difficult for the au pairs:

Samuel: 'We have seen how fast the children forget about
            them [laughs]. [...] But, sometimes, you notice that
            the au pairs become a bit offended, almost hurt by
            [...] how the children don't connect with them
            emotionally.'
Researcher: 'When they leave?'
Samuel: 'Yes, when they leave, for example. Yes, they just say,
            like, "OK, bye, bye".'
Stina: 'And they don't cry. [...]'
Samuel: 'But we have noticed that, in some ways, the au pairs
            feel a bit replaceable. And you don't want it to be

	like that, of course. [...] It is understandable; these au pairs have spent more time with our children, often, at least during the weekdays, more time than we do.'
Researcher:	'But do the children stay in contact with them afterwards?'
Stina:	'No.'

Despite generally downplaying the problem, many parents, while not reflecting that much on the feelings of the nanny or the au pair, do think that the break-ups can be a bit difficult for the children, and also take precautions to make the transitions easier. Many stress the importance of staying in contact, but most tell of difficulties in keeping it up over the long run. It often "fades out", as Leif concludes.

The rather relaxed attitude towards both closeness and break-ups between nannies, au pairs and their children could possibly be related to the fact that Swedish parents, as compared to parents in other national contexts, have more, and historically longer, experience of leaving children in the care of others since most children spend time in daycare centres. Compared to, for example, the US, caring seems to be less loaded with the cultural baggage of the primacy of the mother–child bond and 'blanket accountability'; the assumption that the mother's absence is depriving to their children and might deeply and negatively affect the children's development (Macdonald, 2010: 21). The parents in our sample are not afraid that their children will be harmed by being taken care of by someone else, and neither are they particularly worried that their primary position in the lives of their children will be threatened. Care relations between nannies, au pairs and children are not counted on as lasting for long, which strengthens the position of the parents: despite their not spending as much time with the children in the everyday sense, they are the 'constant' in the child's world. The parents with experience of hiring many nannies and au pairs all see the learning process on the part of the children: while it might be difficult in the beginning, children eventually stop forming close bonds, according to the parents.

Blurry boundaries: employee or family member

When reflecting explicitly upon the role and position of the nanny and the au pair, historical discourses on domestic work in Sweden emerge and become the backdrop against which the parents position themselves. Certain terminology recurs in the interviews, with words such as "*tjänstehjon*", "*hembiträde*" and "*tjänstefolk*", all in different ways signifying 'servants' with a strongly subordinated status, and always used with a disidentificatory purpose: the parents *do not* see their nanny or au pair as a servant or the like. That they feel a need to distance themselves from this image can be interpreted both as an awareness of the negative discursive baggage of paid domestic work in Sweden (as discussed in Chapter 1), and as an awareness of the actual possibility that other people may view their nanny or au pair as a 'servant'. It can also be interpreted as an awareness of the similarity between the actual work that some nannies and au pairs do and the work that was previously performed by 'servants' or 'maids'. Still, finding an appropriate term for this person is difficult, and most parents find themselves negotiating between the positions of 'employed' and 'part of the family'.

(Uncomfortably) employed

Some of the parents argue that they look upon their nanny or au pair mostly as an employee. Jessica (a mother of four), for example, is very upfront with the interviewer when she admits that, actually, she did not want an au pair in the sense of having someone to take care of her children: she wanted a housekeeper. However, it is "deeply rooted in your brain", she says, that you cannot have a housekeeper. So, she hired an au pair and she sees her as "an extra pair of arms" who "facilitates my life so that I can spend more time with my children", an adult, as she says, who can step in when "things get too hectic". Contrary to most parents, she is not interested in her children forming a close relationship with the au pair; neither does she want one herself. However, although she did try to limit the au pair's doings to more closely align with those of a housekeeper, the au pair has been given some responsibility for taking care of the children too, and has formed bonds with them. Still, Jessica would never say that the au pair is even close to being 'part of the family'. Jessica and a few other parents in the study see their au pairs primarily as filling a 'function' in their lives, ready to step in if needed. They are not that interested in the au pair as a person – not that they do not care at all about her well-being, but they are upfront with this being a minor interest. Kicki also sees the au pair as primarily 'an employee', and thinks that the ideal of 'part of the family' that is held by many families and au pairs is unrealistic:

Kicki: 'Many people say that an au pair should be like one
                of the family, but very few Swedes really want that.
                People I know who have au pairs, they don't want

that, and I think that when we realised that too, it was a relief, that you could make that clear from the start, that, "No, we won't be spending time with you in our spare time. When we get home from work, then we take over the children, and you can leave". Then it's not everyone together; then we want to spend time alone with the children.'

Researcher: 'Then it is only you. Do you think that many au pairs expect that, or...?'

Kicki: 'Yes, I think that all the younger girls especially ... they want to be part of a family. They want to be like an older sister in the family, and that is just more of a hassle for me ... because there is so much going on, so many worries, oh my, oh my.... I do think many au pairs want that; they want to be part of the family. It's their dream.... The au pairs want it to be cosy and everything and think that the host family wants an au pair because it is cosy, but that's not really the case.... Most parents want to be alone with their children.'

While not wanting a close relationship with the au pair for herself, Kicki is well aware that her children see the current au pair, Katja, as a member of the family. When the children talk about family, "It is always, 'mummy, daddy, plus Katja'", she says; "They think she is part of the family". Kicki knows that her own position is diametrically opposite to her children's view of their relationship to the au pair: to Kicki, she is "absolutely not", while to the children, she is definitely a family member. However, Kicki is not worried that the au pair will become too close to her children. She thinks that it is good that they have her to confide in, but since she is soon quitting, and Kicki does not plan to stay in contact with her, she is convinced that the children will not miss her. Children "adapt easily" to new situations, she says.

A couple of other parents argue that they see their nannies as employees but on grounds that are very different to those of Jessica and Kicki. For Hilda (a mother of two), to see the nanny as an employee does not feel 'right' for various reasons, but she still tries to do so in order to pay respect to the position of the nanny:

'It sounds so denunciatory to call her an employee. She is, in a way, somehow.... But I don't know. I am ... I'm myself in the world of consultants, so if you compare, it feels like a consult thing, really, because she is employed by the RUT agency, and we have an agreement with them, and then you have to respect each other's working situation, kind of. Because it doesn't feel like she is our employee. She is employed by the agency, and that gives her somehow a higher position and status. You have to negotiate things, not just order her to do things.'

Similarly, Darina also has trouble seeing the nannies that she has hired as employees, but she really tries to keep it that way since she thinks that starting to treat her as one of the family would put the nanny under pressure: it might make her feel obliged to spend time with the family, for fear of them not giving her more work.

Darina and Hilda take a position that is common among nannies and au pairs who have long experience of working in the occupation: to safeguard their working rights and avoid exploitation, for example, to avoid the nanny feeling obligated to spend time with the family when she is off work, regarding the job as 'just a job' is often seen as necessary. However, neither Darina nor Hilda is satisfied with this position; they feel as if their attitude is simultaneously protective *and* downgrading of their nannies.

Absolutely part of the family

Another group of parents take the direct opposite position: to them, the nanny or au pair is part of the family. For some, this is an explicit ideal, something that they strive for and try to create in their everyday interaction with a nanny or an au pair. This is the case for Ingvar and Ingrid. Their needs and expectations of their au pairs have been vast: apart from detailing their work in a schedule that exceeds the 25-hour limit, the au pair is also expected to be social with the parents and keep them company in the evenings. To Ingvar and Ingrid, the au pair is like a family member. They are very pleased with their current au pair, who they think has adapted well to this situation, and who is willing to be flexible, in contrast to a previous au pair who guarded her hours. In framing this quality, they use and refer to family terminology: the current au pair is "like an extra daughter to us", and they try to take her on like "a real member of the family". For Ingvar and Ingrid, to have an au pair is to "invite someone into your life", and the fact that she is living in the house means that she gets to see things normally not shared with people outside of the family:

Ingvar:	'We confide in her a lot when it comes to the home. We invite her to our home […] she is welcomed into our lives, with all that comes with that. We invite her, we almost always have dinner together with her, if she wants to. And it can be like, if we plan a Saturday evening dinner all of us together, "Jenny [au pair], do you want to eat together with us tonight?" and maybe have a glass of wine, and then later on we watch TV, and then maybe she is on her Facebook or Snapchat, but still, she is together with us, in the same room. And then maybe I put one of the children to bed, maybe another child is doing something else, and then the little one wakes up and has dropped her pacifier, well, then Jenny goes to her and gives her the pacifier and maybe lifts her up and comforts her…. She doesn't change diapers when she is off duty, but she does everything else. She does that. And we are trying really, like, "Let me take her now", but she helps out, she helps out.'
Ingrid:	'She does that on her own initiative.'
Ingvar:	'Yes. She is so sweet to the children, all the time, genuinely.'
Ingrid:	'But it is not like we are taking advantage of her. I don't think we are. We are not, like, exploiting her in any way.'

Like many other parents, Ingvar and Ingrid are very careful to let the interviewer know that they are in no way forcing the au pair to do the extra jobs that she is actually doing; it is all on her "own initiative", and she is "genuinely" fond of the children. At the same time, when talking about other au pairs who guarded their working hours and did not want to spend evenings on the sofa with the family, who "locked themselves into their rooms", they made very clear that these au pairs were not living up to the expectations of the family and were not as good as the ones who became 'part of the family' in the way that Ingvar and Ingrid expected.

For Ingvar and Ingrid, the 'part of the family' attitude is related to ideas of availability: they want the au pair to spend as much time as possible with the family. However, the interaction is on terms set by the family as the au pair is supposed to adjust to the family's schedule, including both stepping in to babysit at times when she is off duty and sharing Saturday night dinners and evenings on the sofa. Other families also have a 'part of the family' attitude but put more emphasis on the reciprocity of the arrangement. Ofelia and Olof, for example, are the one couple in our sample that has taken the 'cultural exchange' element in au pairing most seriously. For them, having an au pair is not only a way of 'solving the jigsaw puzzle of life', but also an undertaking on the part of the family to introduce the au pair to Sweden and to their extended family, as well as an opportunity to get to know the au pair's home country by making visits after the au pair has gone back home.

While defining it differently, for Ingvar and Ingrid as well as for Olof and Ofelia, the 'part of the family' position is an explicit ideal. For others, it is more of a consequence following a particular experience. Filippa and her family are an example of this. RUT nannies are less often described in terms of being 'part of the family' than are au pairs, something that is not surprising as they do not live together with the family, and they often spend fewer hours per week in a particular family. However, as our interviews with nannies will show in Chapter 4, many nannies also think of themselves in terms of being 'part of the family', and so do some parents. Filippa has hired many nannies and au pairs over the years, but one nanny stands out. She worked in the family, on and off, for more than three years. During some periods, the family's needs were vast, so the nanny worked in parallel with other girls, but she was always the favourite. Now she has quit but still stays in close contact with the family: "She is just the best ever, she's a rock", Filippa says; "She is part of the family, absolutely".

As with Olof and Ofelia's situation, there is a reciprocity in the relationship between this 'favourite' nanny and the family: the family is now taking part in her life, even outside of work, and Filippa is convinced that the children and the nanny will always stay in touch. This is not at all the case with the rest of the nannies and au pairs who have been part of the children's lives, and Filippa is not really convinced that she would have wanted that either. When Filippa is asked about her hopes for the current au pair, she is "realistic", she says. Although she would wish for this to happen, she does not really expect anyone to be able to fill the shoes of the favourite: "It's kind of unfair to them, really, because … you don't give them a fair chance in that sense".

"This strange hybrid" of employee and family

Most parents in our study never reach a clear position on who the nanny/ au pair is, but waver between seeing her as an employee and as 'part of the family'. In the interviews, they reflect on and negotiate the position of their nannies and au pairs, and have a hard time settling on what they think is a suitable solution. Samuel and Stina end up labelling it as "this strange hybrid, someone who partly works for you but then also is partly a family member". Tomas, who has experience of employing both nannies and au pairs, tries to find a suitable label by comparing their positions with other categories, both those related to employment and those related to friendship and kinship relations:

Tomas: 'It is a different kind of relationship. They are like, they become more like acquaintances and friends, but it feels like they are an adult friend rather than a bigger sister or something. I don't know. Maybe it is different if you have that all "watching TV on the sofa" and "sitting at the dinner table together" relationship....'

Researcher: 'Yes, like part of the family....'

Tomas: 'Yes, even more like part of the family, exactly, maybe.'

Researcher: 'So, you see the au pair as an employee, is that right, or...?'

Tomas: 'Yes, like ... like....'

Researcher: 'Or...?'

Tomas: 'No, but actually, yes, but ... what is an employee, really? After all, this is someone we have a much closer relationship with – the au pair is much closer to us than the preschool teachers, right? But in a way, the preschool teachers are employed by the daycare centre. But absolutely, there is an element of that since she is not together with us all the time, all the meals, she's not spending time with us on the weekends.'

Tomas cannot find a definition of her position that he feels comfortable with: she is neither an employee nor part of the family. On a previous occasion, he also compared her to the cleaner that the family employs: "That is a different kind of relationship; that's like buying a service". Having a nanny or an au pair is "inviting someone into your home, and yes, of course, that's buying a service too, but it is more like ... our au pair, she is actually coming here to help us with our children". Tomas is simultaneously rejecting and confirming the view of their nannies and au pairs as providing a 'service', and, in the end, what seems to be the qualitative difference in his mind is the character of what they do. The 'service' cannot really be seen as a service because of the content: taking care of children.

Ann-Katrin and Arvid also shift between different definitions in their interview. However, their ambivalence is more related to their descriptions of actual doings: their au pairs are positioned as employees on some occasions during the interview and as part of the family on others. At the beginning of the interview, Ann-Katrin makes it very clear that she is not interested in hiring au pairs who are looking for cultural exchange. Some girls who want to be au pairs think that they will be like exchange students, Ann-Katrin says, but she has learned to state this early: "They are here to make our life easier; they are like our elastic band, kind of". However, when describing different situations and occasions in their lives with au pairs, both arguments – about being 'part of the family' and about being 'an employee' – occur and serve different purposes. On one occasion, for instance, Ann-Katrin and Arvid describe the family routine in the evening. The au pair's chores for the day are first described as ending at dinner, but then the au pair is still expected to "help out" as part of the "family responsibility".

Ann-Katrin:	'The grown-ups that are at home help out, contribute to get food on the table. [...] And if it is all three of us, then it doesn't take long. But you could say that her responsibility ends when we've finished our dinner. But, sometimes, it could be that I do the dishes, and she goes upstairs and starts getting the children into their pyjamas, but, in principle, it is ... she is off duty after dinner. But it is the shared family responsibility to empty and load the dishwasher ... and take out the trash and things like that.'
Arvid:	'But, sometimes, when you are not home, then she helps to put the children to bed, sometimes, but not always. It is kind of floating; it's not something we demand, but sometimes she does that too.'

The "shared family responsibility" of the grown-ups who are at home becomes the argument that makes the au pair's working day "floating" and expanding into more chores. "In principle", she is off duty at dinner, but then she enters into another category of being part of the family, and, as such, she is expected to "help out".

Ann-Katrin and Arvid's case shows that the lack of resolution between the two definitions of 'part of the family' and 'employee' can give the host parents the advantage of defining it according to their own needs. Their narrative is a common one in literature on paid domestic work, as discussed in Chapter 2 (Anderson, 2000). However, most parents – including Ann-Katrin and Arvid – are, indeed, genuinely concerned with how to label, and also how to treat, their nannies and au pairs so that they do not feel 'used' or exploited. The difficulty in finding a suitable definition of the role attests to this, as do at least some parents' attempts to form a more reciprocal relationship with their nannies and au pairs. However, it is as if the practice itself does not fit in: defining her as an 'employee', even when it is done in the spirit of respect for the nanny's/au pair's position as a worker, feels as inadequate as defining her as 'part of the family'. Tomas's hesitancy of calling care for children a service is indicative: there seems to be something in the 'doing' of care for children that makes it hard to pin down and define.

Conclusion: buying time to parent

Delegating care to a nanny or an au pair is a practice that brings many gains, according to the parents we interviewed. Gender-equality ideals of dual-earner – although not dual-carer – families can be realised, and women are able to enter into careers as challenging and time-consuming as men's. Most importantly, the 'jigsaw puzzle of life' is solved. The presence of a nanny or an au pair, and her doing of care around children and in the home, relieves the parents of responsibilities and 'buys them time': time to work, but also time *not to do* certain parts of the care work at home. The nanny and the au pair enables 'quality time', both through enhancing and enriching the time she spends with the children (engaging with them and filling their leisure time with qualitative activities), and also through doing the boring, mundane things that the parents do not have time to do – and sometimes do not want to do themselves. She takes the stress out of the everyday. She becomes the "elastic band", she takes on the "buffer time" or, as we will suggest later on in Chapters 6 and 7, her doings become an *invisible glue* that binds the family together and thereby enables the realisation of (partly transformed) ideals of gender equality, good parenting and, more generally, a good family life.

However, while the parents can quite easily identify and talk about the gains of inviting nannies and au pairs into the family, talk about the actual doings of nannies and au pairs is more ambiguous. The process of delegating care is handled differently by all the parents, as are the counting of hours and the parents' expectations of what nannies and au pairs should actually do in the family. Despite attempts to nail down and be clear about what they expect from her, there still seems to be something indeterminable in the practice of care around children as such. The 'good nanny/au pair' does not merely do the agreed-upon tasks; she does more. She 'sees' what needs to be done, and she 'takes initiative'. The 'easy' chores of nannying and au pairing turn out to be quite complex indeed. The ambiguity is also reflected in the difficulty that most parents encounter in trying to define 'who she is': neither the label 'employee' nor that of 'part of the family' fits. It is also visible in the ambiguousness that comes out when reflecting upon the relationship between the nanny, au pair and the child: on the one hand, there is an expectation of closeness; on the other, there is an unpreparedness or unwillingness to assure that this close relationship is safeguarded, as seen in the downplaying of the importance of break-ups and staying in contact. This kind of 'nanny circle' that the child is supposed to handle – welcoming nannies and au pairs, getting to know them, saying goodbye, and then welcoming again – prevents the care relationship between the nanny/au pair and the child from becoming too close. Joan Tronto (2002: 40) has argued that nanny and au pair care fosters an attitude of exchangeability, that children learn to treat 'people as means, not as ends in themselves'. When parents expect and count on their children to learn the 'system' of nannies and au pairs coming and going, this ethos is, indeed, present.

Each parent that we interviewed never doubted their position as the primary and most important person in the lives of their children. That nannies and au pairs come and go is built into the very arrangement of the practice, but the parents remain. This gives them an overarching responsibility and a position of being in control and orchestrating the caring framework in which nannies, au pairs and children find themselves. Although all parents in our study are still engaged in doing everyday care chores – some more than others – there are assumptions about the possibility of dividing care into 'spiritual' and 'menial' doings that emerge in the parents' talk: while some things can more easily be delegated, other things are 'valued highly' because they are 'thought to be essential to the proper functioning of the household and the moral upbringing of children' (Roberts, 1997: 51). In addition, the mundane care doings can occasionally become 'spiritual' when carried out by a parent and when the stress and necessity of doing is gone. This prompts us to ask: what does parenting become, then, when everyday mundane doings of care are delegated? We will return to this question in our final chapter.

4

Nannies and Au Pairs
Doing Care

Gloria

The first time we meet with Gloria, a 20-year-old au pair from the US, she is bubbly and talkative and has a very positive attitude towards almost everything, especially so towards her Swedish host family. At this point, Gloria had spent two months in the family, and she immediately starts talking about how much she loves her work, how she likes spending time outdoors with the children and how she and the host mother sometimes go shopping together. It was an instant match, she says; when they spoke on Skype before she came, she says that she could already "tell they were just warm and friendly". Gloria arrived in Sweden on a Sunday afternoon, got introduced to the work by the mother on the following Monday and then started to work – on her own – on the Tuesday. Her working tasks include taking care of the family's three children and doing household chores. Both her host mother and her host father work full time and are really busy, she tells the interviewer; in fact, thinking about it, she cannot understand how they managed before she arrived. In the morning Gloria gets the children ready for school and daycare and makes sure they get there in time. When she gets back again, she cleans up after breakfast, she makes the beds, and occasionally vacuums. After that she takes the dog for a walk and sometimes also goes grocery shopping. Twice a week, Gloria attends a Swedish-language school in town, paid for by the parents. Around 4.00 pm, she picks up the children, takes them to their different and plentiful after-school activities, such as tennis, horseback riding, music lessons and swimming classes, helps them with their homework, and sometimes also cooks dinner for the whole family.

In the evenings and on the weekends, she often spends time together with the family.

Living in the house makes her "part of the family", she says; her being there and being around means that the parents get some much-needed extra help, even if it is past her working hours. She does not mind helping out – "it just seems natural", she says. Sometimes, she does some extra cleaning, and she also often takes care of the children on her time off: "I don't feel like I am working", "I just may have been very lucky; I have a very relaxed family". Getting to know the children was a lot easier than she had imagined, but also a little bit hard since they did not speak the same language. Gloria tells us that she is still in the process of trying to figure out her relationship to the children and emphasises that she really wants to build a good connection with them over the months to come.

When we meet Gloria a couple of months later, things are different. Almost immediately, she starts telling about the difficulties she has experienced with her family recently. One morning before work, her host father told her that she was not doing enough activities together with the children. If the family was to have an au pair, she should not just let them sit with their tablets, he said. This, they could do on the weekends when the parents were at home, but not on weekdays when Gloria was spending time with them. Instead, the parents wanted Gloria to set up more rules for the children, and also to do more qualitative activities such as crafting, baking, outdoor activities and homework. In addition, they wanted her to teach the children English. Gloria felt quite overwhelmed by these requests:

> 'That's another expectation that the parents have [laughing], is that … I construct, like, English lessons for them, but that's not something that I've done and…. How do I – there's just so much other stuff. It's, it's hard to get them to do their homework already, it's hard to keep them on the same activity, to, you know, prepare an afternoon snack, make sure that they're not eating things that they're not supposed to be eating, make sure they're not getting on the iPads…. Like there's, I'm like, where am I supposed to…?'

Objecting to these wishes from the parents was, however, not an option in Gloria's mind. Despite the fact that she was in Sweden legally and that she, speaking English, could make herself understood, she had no one else but the parents to turn to when she felt that her work situation was problematic. In this case, she thought that talking to them about her discomfort might even cause more problems for her since she lives and works in the same house as the family. Instead, Gloria started to compare her own situation to the situation of other au pairs that she has heard about, who were placed in 'bad' families that made them work even more than she had to. Knowing that others were worse off made her think and feel that her situation was not that bad after all.

Not only did Gloria's understanding of the work differ between the two interviews, but so did her talk about her relationship to the children. In the first interview, she talked about this as something that came "naturally". In the second interview, their relationship and how to form her *own* bond with them emerged as more complicated. The parents' views on how she should be with them differed; the father was stricter than the mother, and Gloria tried to position herself somewhere in between. Also, she sometimes disagreed with the parents' way of handling the children, but she still felt that she had to abide by their childrearing strategies. At the same time, she did try to sneak in her own ideas on how to best deal with them, and to act in accordance with what she felt necessary in the different situations she found herself in. The relationship to the parents and their ideas about how she should be and what she should do with the children consequently came out as decisive for how Gloria's relationship with them turned out.

In Gloria's narrative, several elements come out that reoccur in the narratives that we listened to in our interviews with nannies and au pairs. Joy and excitement over working in a family coexists with discomfort of experienced discrepancies between stated working agreements and actual work, and the feeling of being treated as a resource that should be prepared to step in whenever needed. We also see difficulties of finding one's position in the family; eagerness to get to know and become close to the children is coupled with difficulties in finding a way to care for them that is considered 'good' by both the parents and the children, and that also corresponds with one's own experience of what constitutes a good way to deal with care situations. To negotiate this, to 'read' and to handle a situation in a way that makes all parties happy, is a necessary, but delicate, task. In this chapter, we will zoom in on nannies and au pairs working in Swedish families, and on the care situation that they become part of, and create, in everyday life.

Nannying and au pairing in Sweden

For decades, working as a nanny or an au pair has been uncommon in Sweden. The reoccurrence of the nanny profession is, as we argued in Chapter 1, closely related to the introduction of the tax deduction on household services in 2007. Since then, the nanny market has grown rapidly and, parallel to this, a market for au pairs has arisen.

In many ways, nanny and au pair jobs are similar. The 26 nannies and au pairs that we met with in this study all care for somebody else's children within the home setting of the employing family. However, the framework of their work differs. Au pairs like Gloria who are from outside of the European Union (EU) have a work permit issued for one year, if in Sweden legally. Au pairs from within the EU are in Sweden without a work permit. Both groups are employed directly by the parents, and neither category has an official third party to turn to in the event that problematic situations arise.[1] In comparison, nannies are formally employed by nanny agencies, which means that, at least in theory, they have someone to turn to in case a problematic situation arises.[2] Despite this, nannies work under insecure working conditions since they seldom know how many hours they will work each week and for how long the parents will want them to continue working in the family.

The different work arrangements, where the au pairs in our study were living together with the family while the nannies were always 'live-out' and often working only two or three afternoons per week, also affected their situations. It was experienced as more difficult for an au pair to leave her host family if she was not satisfied with the working conditions since her employment was always a private arrangement between her and the parents, and since she knew that leaving would potentially force her to go back to her home country. Several au pairs were also very dependent on their income as they sent remittances back home.

Nannies' and au pairs' different positions also play out in their different reasons for taking on the job (see also Stubberud, 2015; Bikova, 2017). While a few (four) of the au pairs that we met with explained that their main reason for becoming an au pair was to experience a new country and learn Swedish, which can be interpreted as in line with the general idea of au pairing, the majority (11) listed other reasons. Most had unsuccessfully been looking for other jobs, but as they did not find any, and neither a place to live, they ended up as au pairs. Taking work as an au pair also meant that they could improve their Swedish, maybe even get a Swedish social security number and thereby further improve their chances of getting another job in Sweden later on, they argued. In most cases, the nannies, who with a few exceptions were from Sweden, were students in the areas of early childhood education and social work, which set them apart from the au pairs in the sense that they were more often interested in working specifically with children in their future professions.

Turning to the actual practices that nannies and au pairs engage in, it will become clear that despite differences, the experiences of nannies' and au pairs' doings of care in families are very similar. In the next section, we will focus on their understandings of their work tasks, and especially the coexistence of narratives of their work as being 'easy and simple' and reports of practices being much more complex and demanding. Second, we will look more closely at what it means to be in a care situation with children, and how the nannies and au pairs relate to and form bonds with the children in the midst of expectations from parents. Third, and finally, we will turn to the nannies' and au pairs' navigation in finding their role in the family, once again – as in Chapter 3 – drawing on and problematising the categories of 'part of the family' and 'employee'. The function and meaning of narratives of 'being lucky' concludes the chapter, pointing towards an inherent precarity in the practice of nanny and au pair care as it is organised today.

Simple work tasks, complex doings of care and 'reading situations': the nanny and au pair version of the 'jigsaw puzzle of life'

As the parents described in Chapter 3, nannies and au pairs are employed to solve the families' 'jigsaw puzzle of life'. They are their "elastic band", as the mother Ann-Katrin put it, and their main engagement is characterised by the parents in terms placing it at the 'labour/menial' end of the dichotomy (Roberts, 1997). Their work is framed as 'easy' by the parents, and this is, indeed, also reflected in the official framing of the work: the Migration Agency rules for au pairing talk about 'light housework', and nanny work is similarly labelled by the nanny companies as a 'fun' extra job for 'child-loving' young people interested in earning some extra money with no requirements of training. Looking at the narratives of the nannies and au pairs, they also reproduce this image, but, simultaneously, when talking in detail about their actual doings during the day, this gets problematised.

Hours, tasks and flexibility

The image of 'easy and limited' is often reproduced and problematised in the same accounts, for example, when nannies and au pairs talk about their tasks and working hours. The au pair Ellie does this when she is describing her workday:

Ellie:	'I get up at a quarter past six, get ready and then meet the children around seven in the kitchen to make them breakfast and eat with them. And then we go upstairs, I brush their teeth and take them to school.... [...] Then, around half past eight or nine, I'm done with that, and then I have ... sort of free time until four, when I pick them up, and within that time, I have my weekly duties, doing the laundry, grocery shopping and then taking care of the food. [...] I take them home and then it's, yeah ... an hour where we play a bit and I get the food ready, and then at six we all eat together. [...] I set the table and get the food ready, and then we eat, and after that ... I'm sort of done with the day.'
Researcher:	'Do you have to, you know, clear the table and stuff?'
Ellie:	'I clean up in the kitchen, but not alone, we [parents and au pair] sort of do that together.... But a lot of times, the parents, one of them, is not home in the evening, so then I kind of help out getting the kids ready for bed. So, sometimes, it's not that I'm done at half past six – it's more like seven or eight o'clock.'

In talking about her day, Ellie shifts between describing her tasks and engagements as limited, and then recognising their fluidity. Just like the mother Nelly in Chapter 3, when she described her au pair's regular working day, the "free" time during the day turns out to be a time when quite a lot of things need to be done. When Ellie lables this as "*sort of free time*" it shows that, in a sense, she is aware of this too. At the end of the quote, it becomes clear that Ellie is not even sure at what time her workday actually ends: it all depends on the needs of the family. According to their agreement, her workday should be over by dinner, but this is seldom the case due to the parents being away. This way of describing chores is common in the interviews with nannies and au pairs: while starting out by describing well-defined tasks that are done within the designated hours, when giving accounts of actual practices, the tasks are revealed as much more comprehensive and dependent on the families' needs. Among the parents, flexibility is a much sought-after attribute when they look for a nanny or an au pair, both in terms of time (when to work) and in terms of the different tasks they want them to do. The nannies and au pairs experience this in different ways. In some cases, tasks are visibly added, as in the introductory example of Gloria, whose family gradually gave her more tasks to carry out. More often, the nanny and au pair narratives attest to tasks being introduced through implicit expectations: regardless of previous agreements, they are expected to just be there and help out whenever needed.

The need to be flexible comes out clearly in the au pair Irina's narrative. Irina has worked for several families, and in one of them, she became very close to both the child and the mother. While she appreciated this on some levels, she also recognised that it was problematic since it affected her work hours: "Even though I got on so well with her [the mother], she'd take the piss an awful lot.... when I'd, like, in the evenings, she'd say she would be home at seven and she wouldn't come home until ten, by which time I'd put the child to bed". Not knowing when the mother would be home meant that she could never make any evening plans on her own. Although this was not part of their initial agreement, Irina found herself in a situation where she was expected to be home every weekday afternoon, evening and night, always ready to take care of the child. Irina felt that she had to accept the mother's behaviour as their friendship-like relationship made it difficult for her to complain: since they shared a house, Irina was scared that her complaining would cause an awkward situation for them all.

Saying 'no' to added tasks or expectations of flexibility is experienced as very difficult by the nannies and au pairs. Some of the narratives told to us show that the consequences of raising complaints can, indeed, be harsh. One nanny talked about trying to make the parents set up a weekly work schedule for her so that she would know what days she was going to work. The parents in the family had high expectations of flexibility, both in terms of tasks and hours, and they often did not make arrangements until a couple of days ahead. The parents did not appreciate the nanny's request for a schedule: she was consequently dismissed.

Instead of raising complaints, some nannies and au pairs develop strategies. A common way for au pairs to avoid working after hours is, for example, to physically leave the house and choose to not have dinner together with the family and thereby not risk being involved in care activities around and after dinner. However, having conscious strategies is not always possible. Care is, as Wærness (1984) has argued, a practice in which the unexpected is always there in the background. This means that it is impossible to tell beforehand what is going to happen, how the person you are taking care of will react and whether one's handling of the situation will work out as planned.

Narratives about handling the unexpected turn up in all the interviews. The case of the nanny Andrea is illustrative in this respect. When we met her for the first time, she talked about her job, which she had only just started, as being "rather easy". Similar to the other nannies and au pairs, she presented her work tasks in a straightforward manner: to pick up the children from school and daycare, take them to activities, play with them, and cook dinner for them. She liked the family and the children, and she felt happy and satisfied. When we met again a month later for a second interview, and after Andrea had kept a diary for a week, her feelings and understandings of her work were very different. One particular incident had changed her understanding of the work. In her diary, she wrote:

> Today I worked between 15.30 and 19.30, which means an hour over time. I picked up the kids and we had a quick snack at home before we went to the older son's football practice. I was pretty nervous, because I did not know if I would find the way there, but it went ok. The children were happy in the beginning, but then the youngest girl got really tired [and fell asleep in the car], and when we went to pick up the oldest one again, and I woke her up, she got really upset. I do not think that I have ever felt as awful as when I was carrying the screaming child out of the car. [...] The day was really hard. I was totally knocked out when I got back home, and I was so relieved when their mother came home and I could bike back to my place. I do not know if there was anything that made me happy today. It was the worst day at work so far. I guess I will learn about the little one's mood swings and then will not feel as bad next time it happens.

In the interview, Andrea expanded further on what happened: "The other parents at the sports centre were staring at me, and I just.... 'She is tired today'", she says; "I felt almost like a kidnapper". While the incident made Andrea feel bad at the time, she also felt that she actually did not know how to handle the child. She was left to figure this out in the moment, and afterwards, she was unsure whether she had handled it in the right way or not. Andrea tried to talk to the mother about this but the mother was busy and just stated that she should not have let the child fall asleep, advice that Andrea was dissatisfied with. Andrea felt that she needed more guidance, but she was reluctant to discuss the situation with the parents again. Doing so would mean that she exposed her insecurity about how to handle different situations, and she feared that she would appear to be a 'bad nanny': "I have done this before; it should not be a problem", she says, but she is still left with a feeling of not being able to do her job well enough. She recognises in the interview that the job of a nanny is a lot more difficult and demanding than she had expected, and that neither the parents nor the agency had prepared her for that.

The nannies' and au pairs' narratives about their everyday work activities reveal that care work is hardly ever the thought-to-be ideal activity: the 'unexpected' is always lurking in the background, popping up in different forms in relation to different actors and activities. However, the unexpected is not, at least at first, thought of as being part of the care situation; rather, it is narrated as distinct events, separate from ideas of how things ideally 'should be', although, in reality, things hardly ever go as planned. It is also evident that flexibility, in hours and tasks, while not being part of the initial characterisation of nannying and au pairing, is present, both in parents' expectations and also necessary in itself, since this is what is required for a care situation to be 'good'. The 'solving of the jigsaw puzzle' requires much more than the imagined 'menial' tasks; it involves very complex emotional doings on the part of nannies and au pairs, of being attuned to and reading the situation (Mason, 1996). This will emerge with more clarity when we turn our focus towards stress and 'quality time'.

Stress and quality time

An important way in which nannies and au pairs are thought to solve the parents' 'jigsaw puzzle of life' is to reduce not only the daily stress experienced by the parents themselves, but also the stress that the parents feel that they induce in their children. Having a nanny or an au pair makes possible a more stress-free everyday life for all, they argue. This image is confirmed by some nannies and au pairs, who told us about being amazed by the parents being so calm and patient with the children, despite their working so much. The au pair Kate's description of her host family's weekday mornings attests to the possibilities emerging when there is someone else there to do the necessary chores: when Kate takes care of the practicalities of preparing and cleaning up after breakfast, the children play the piano together with the parents before they head off to work and school.

Most narratives of morning routines told to us by au pairs (as they are more commonly working in the morning, as compared to nannies) were significantly more complex, and also, in fact, filled with descriptions of stress. Stress may have been reduced for the parents, but it was instead experienced and handled by the nannies and au pairs. The au pair Caroline's narrative is illustrative in this respect. In the interview with her host parents, they had expressed lots of worries and a guilty conscience for letting their stressful lives affect their children, and vividly described the situation before hiring nannies and au pairs: getting into fights in the morning, or at pick-up at daycare in the afternoon, and the significant reduction of stress in everyday life that having nannies and au pairs meant to them. However, for Caroline, things are not as unproblematic:

> 'It's a little bit hard to work with [the children] because sometimes they don't agree or something, and sometimes I don't know what to do with them, but because sometimes they have some stress, they yell and.... Yeah, and today it was the problem when we went to the daycare. The child didn't want to go inside and he cried all the time, and I couldn't do anything. I said, "Please, go inside, you need to go to daycare", but he cried and didn't want to, and I thought that maybe we should go back home or, or maybe it is not a good idea.'

The parents' image of the new situation is that of stress-free mornings and calm and cosy afternoons at home; in the eyes of Caroline, this is not the case. Instead, Caroline is now handling the children's outbursts, yelling and crying, and doing this is, indeed, difficult work.

While au pairs often talk about handling stressful mornings, the afternoons – when nannies are at work too – can also be experienced as very intense. As we saw in the parents' accounts, this was a time that they often wished to escape, a 'critical moment', when everyone is tired and hungry, and all the mundane everyday chores have to be taken care of. In the parents' narratives, there is little reflection on how this time is experienced by the nannies, au pairs and children. In the nannies'/ au pairs' interviews – as well as in the children's interviews, as we will see in Chapter 5 – this time comes out as crucial indeed, but also as a time marked by difficult emotional doings. In the words of the nanny Petra:

> 'Sometimes, it can be a bit stressful, like if I pick the children up late and it takes a lot of time and so on. And then maybe I have 45 minutes before the parents get home, and then I am supposed to cook dinner for the children, make sure that they are busy doing something while I am doing that. They are going to eat, and then the parents want me to clean up after them as well. But, I usually try to get them involved in cooking dinner, or I try to, like boiling the water and stuff, while I might go get pens and papers and help them a little, so you have to like multitask a bit.'

In addition to relating very similar experiences to those of the parents – of handling tired children and juggling multiple tasks at the same time

– the nannies and au pairs often, like Petra, worry about making sure that everything is done before the parents come home: that the afternoon snack has been served, that homework is done, that 'qualitative activities' have taken place and that dinner is started (and sometimes served).

To be able to handle stressful times during the afternoon, the nannies and au pairs have different strategies. One common strategy is to let the children watch television or play with tablets. While some host parents were fine with them handling a hectic or problematic situation in this way, others, like Gloria's host parents in the introductory story, thought that this went against their idea of the qualitative activities that they had hired her to do with the children. Another strategy, often meeting with greater parental approval, is to do as Petra describes in the preceding quote and let the children join in preparing food. However, this can also be stressful in itself: having children near the stove can feel dangerous and requires very good multitasking abilities, as Petra recognises. Likewise, baking cookies, an activity that parents approve of and, as we will see, often appreciated by children, can also be experienced as complex: while some nannies and au pairs think that it is an enjoyable joint activity, others find it stressful and talk about having to handle conflicts between siblings over who gets to do what, and over the mess in the kitchen that they have to deal with afterwards. Some nannies and au pairs even admit that they find baking boring, although this is not something they tell either parents or children. Stress, then, is not only about making sure that things are done before a particular time, but can also be part of the actual activity; something that is supposed to be fun from the point of view of the parents can be experienced as quite demanding in practice.

As we saw in the parents' narratives, one positive outcome of employing a nanny or an au pair is that it enables more 'quality time' for them and their children. The au pairs and nannies are often very aware of their role in this and know that they are needed to make everyday life work. However, creating the possibility of 'good family life' is not only about relieving the parents of mundane everyday tasks; it also involves a more direct creation of 'family time' on behalf of the nannies and au pairs. This is visible in talk about when and where they should be present. The au pair Ellie, for example, has developed a sense of where in the house she should be: one of the floors in the family's huge home where she works is the family's space, and while she is allowed there, and, indeed, needs to be there on some occasions to be able to do her job, she has also developed a sense of when *not* to go there, when she should leave the family alone. The host mother is very happy with her ability to "read different situations", says Ellie, not only flexibility regarding work hours and tasks, but also her ability to sense when she should withdraw.

Indeed, developing this sense can be crucial for keeping one's job. Olivia, who now works as an au pair in her third family, talks about how she has learned this the hard way. In the first family she worked for, she got so close to the children that the mother, after just four months, wanted her to leave the family as she felt threatened by Olivia's bond with the children. In the family that Olivia works for now, she tries to keep some distance therefore:

> 'If both parents are home, I try to keep my distance more, so I don't … play with the kids unless they ask me to. […] Or, for example, sometimes on the weekends, if the children ask me, "Oh, can you play a round of Uno with me?", I'm not gonna say "no" because that would hurt their feelings, but on the weekend, I try to not interact with the children as much because then they know, now it's parents' time. […] I'm still there, and I'm still helping because I'm still at my workplace, but I try to just give them some family time.'

Just as the nanny's and au pair's privacy becomes subject to the gaze of family members, one can argue that the family is also exposed to the gaze of the employed domestic worker (Búriková and Miller, 2010: 34). However, there is a fundamental inequality in the parties' possibilities of handling the knowledge of private life: while parents have greater means to delineate and control the levels of closeness, nannies and au pairs have to carefully use their knowledge to keep their status as 'good' in the eyes of the parents, for example, through knowing when to withdraw in order to create 'family time'. Children, on the other hand, have comparably limited possibilities of guarding their privacy, as we will discuss in Chapter 5.

Nannies' and au pairs' doings take place in the midst of their relationship to the children and to the parents. In addition to doing the more defined designated tasks of cleaning, doing laundry and helping children with their homework, the 'menial' and easy chores that parents wish to be relieved from so that they can engage in 'spiritual' activities in quality time when they get home (Roberts, 1997), nannies and au pairs need to engage in lots of different emotional activities (Mason, 1996). The underlying understanding of their work as easy and limited is constantly being interrupted and questioned by experiences of the need to be flexible, both in hours and tasks, and in being put in actual situations that – contrary to parents' ideas – are still full of stress. To be able to handle uncooperative children, unexpected events or stressful situations requires both hard practical work and the ability to 'read' complex situations, as well as to act upon a situation in a way that is considered 'good' by the parents and that works for the children and themselves. To be able to do this reading in a way that the parents approve of, they need to have knowledge about the family so that they can sense their wishes and needs and can act accordingly (DeVault, 1991). In some cases, these emotional doings even seem to have become embodied. As the au pair Ellie says at one point in the interview, she has started to think and feel like a mother as she has in her mind everything that needs to be done. She does not have to be told, she 'just knows' (DeVault, 1991).

Being in care situations with children

The nannies' and au pairs' 'solving of the jigsaw puzzle' involves handling the expectations on themselves, defined both by the framework of nannying and au pairing, and by more concrete expectations – implicit and explicit – placed on them by the parents. All of this is to be enacted in the actual care situation she finds herself in, together with the children. Carving out ways of doing care in this situation is often a complex enterprise, where the relationship that one might think should be the most important one – that between nanny/au pair and child – is not always at the centre.

Balancing expectations

Getting to know a new family and their children takes time and effort and involves a lot of trying to figure out the family's routines and how they want things to be done. It requires of the nanny or the au pair that she figure out how she should be with the children through learning about the children's needs, what they like and do not like, and also what the parents expect of them, and what they themselves think is a good way of handling a situation. This is a balancing act that requires quite a lot of effort, and nannies and au pairs talk about different ways of handling the situations they find themselves in. Many talk about being insecure of whether they are 'doing it right' in the eyes of the parents. The au pair Caroline, for example, is very concerned with the parents' lack of response to her way of dealing with the children in her care:

> 'It's not easy, and sometimes I don't know what to do when
> the parents, they sit with us and watch how I speak with
> the children, and sometimes I need to be firm with them,
> but sometimes I'm afraid to be firm with them because the

parents, they look at me, and I don't know – is it normal or is it not normal? And I don't know, maybe they want that I am sometimes firm with them, but maybe they don't want that I am firm with them, but they don't.... They didn't tell me what I need to do. It's a bit of a problem for me.'

The parents' lack of response makes her worried, and the insecurity that comes out of this affects her doings with the children even when the parents are not physically present, which was also visible in the earlier quote about her trying to handle a child refusing to go to daycare. While she does, indeed, have her own ideas of a solution to the situation, she feels uncertain as to whether the parents would approve of this.

While some mostly talk about 'doing it right' in the eyes of the parents, others focus more on the children in their interviews. Olivia, for example, is very aware of the importance of getting the children's trust and the need to navigate between showing the children that she really cares for them and, at the same time, gaining the parents' trust that she is capable of handling the situation:

'Of course, in the beginning, it's sometimes a little strange because you are basically a big part of their life but you don't know them and they don't know you, so it takes some time to get them to trust you. But I feel with the children, that it goes a lot quicker than with ... adults. I think you just have to listen to what they say to you, so they just really come close to you and ... try to get to know them. And I feel like, if they feel that you are, that you care about them, then they open up really quickly.... I experience that children are always very willing to open up to you and ... but it's also important that you get some support from the parents because I have had it both ways. In my current family, the parents support me; they tell the children that if I'm there, I'm the leader [laughing], so I'm the person of authority and that if I say something, then the parents support me.'

Olivia acknowledges that getting to know the children takes time and effort, and this is the basis for making the whole care situation work. In addition, for the care situation to be good, her way of dealing with the children needs to have support from the parents. As indicated in the quote, Olivia experiences support from her current employer, but she also has experience of working in families where this did not happen, where the parents undermined and questioned her way of dealing with the children instead.

When views diverge, nannies and au pairs find strategies to handle the discrepancy between what they find necessary in the care situation and what parents expect. Cilla, for example, has experiences of working as a nanny in several families at the same time, and in the beginning, she was frustrated with them having different childrearing ideas: some corresponded well with her own view of how to handle care situations and others did not. For example, she realised that the families had very different ideas about children's use of electronic devices. To manage the situation, Cilla came to the conclusion that she should disregard her own views on the matter and just do what each family wanted her to:

> 'In the beginning, or before, I sometimes thought it was really difficult that you had to, kind of, *learn* the family and sometimes your own views were different from theirs. [...] At one point, I realised that I should just do things the way the family wants me to do. One of the families I worked for had really strict rules when it came to computers and TV, while the other did not have any at all. And I have also my own ideas, like I think you should have pretty strict rules. [...] After a while, I got a bit more relaxed in one of the families and a bit stricter in the other one [...] to a certain extent. Because there are some things I wouldn't accept.' (Emphasis added)

Cilla has adopted a strategy of adjusting to the parents' rules, or lack of them, but she still talks about bringing in her own childrearing ideas and, most importantly, she does what she thinks is necessary to create a good care situation. She does this in a non-confrontational way through sneaking in suggestions of activities that she thinks makes the care situation better for all. For example, in the family with no rules for the use of electronic devices, she thinks that the children get whiny and irritated if they sit by their computers all afternoon, so she has come up with ways to make the care situation better: she has learned that they really like to be on the trampoline, so she "lures them into" physical activity, as she says, by suggesting this. For similar reasons, she has introduced board games to get them off their computers and make them spend some more time together. This has paid off, she says, as she and the youngest boy have developed a close relationship over time. He now wants to spend one-to-one time with her and misses her if she is not there on her regular days. She also cares for him, is happy when she sees him and misses him when she is not there.

Many of the nannies and au pairs were concerned about not causing conflict about childrearing strategies since this might change the atmosphere between them and the parents and compromise the good working environment, or even jeopardise their job. When they did not agree with the parents' childrearing strategies, they therefore tried to do things differently, without the parents' knowledge. The nanny Disa, for example, withholds some information from the mother in the family. When Disa's workday is over and the mother comes home again, Disa recounts to her only parts of what has happened during the day:

> 'If I would have told the mother that it has been a pinch-and-pull-the-hair kind of day [...]. Like, "There have been some fights today", then the mother would say to the girl, "Do we need to put you in the corner?". Like, they have this – they are very authoritarian [...] This "time-out" approach, and then I feel like, "Shall I do like that too?" [...] I personally do not believe in that.... But, at the same time, I do not want the girl to think that she can do whatever she wants when she is with me because I do not give her a time out. [...] I feel a little, I can meet the parents' wants in some ways, but in other ways, I can't because I do not want to do something that I do not believe in.'

Disa and the mother disagree on how to discipline a child, and Disa finds her own way of handling the situations without using the authoritarian methods suggested by the mother. By keeping information from the mother, she further protects the child and makes sure that the child is not punished when the mother comes home.

The actual doings of care that come out are consequently negotiated between the parents' expectations and wishes and the children's needs and wants, as well as the nannies' and au pairs' own understandings of what the care situation requires. Their reading of the situation and their suggested solutions are based upon both their previously formed ideas of what 'good care' is, and, most importantly, their knowledge acquired in the specific situation (Wærness, 1984: 197), about what the particular child and the particular moment requires. However, the parents still provide the framework for the nannies' and au pairs' doings, and parents' positionings are always present, sometimes very visibly so, sometimes more obscured. The nannies' and au pairs' doing of care is consequently situational and relational, and while they make space for acting in a way that concurs with their own reading of the care situation, as well as their ideas of what 'good care' is, they still have to negotiate this in relation to the parents.

Distance, closeness and the complexities of leaving

Even though the parents' views of the care practice come out as highly important for the way in which the care practice is played out, there is still, as concluded earlier, space for nannies and au pairs to form a specific relationship to the children within the care situation. In fact, this often emerges as a necessity, as something inevitable when being in a care situation together. Reflections upon distance and closeness in relation to children emerge especially in talk about the fact that the nannies and au pairs know from the outset that they are going to leave the family one day. Engagement of nannies and au pairs is in almost all cases short in Sweden: au pairs are limited by the one-year rule (though these rules are not always followed), and nannies employed by RUT agencies expect to be hired for relatively short-term engagements. Start working for a family, get to know the children and then one day leave and, in many cases, also start working for another family and get to know new children; this scenario is a background condition of the whole practice of nannying and au pairing. It is a 'nanny circle' that affects all involved, but especially so the nannies, au pairs and the children. It is this condition that makes some nannies and au pairs try to keep a distance, and, similarly, what makes children do the same, as we will see in Chapter 5.

The nanny Monika, for example, talks about how she has tried to have an employer–employee relationship with the family that she works for since she does not want to get hurt the day she leaves. She is trying to maintain a distance from the children in her care, but this is hard. She has become very fond of especially one of the children and often thinks about him, even when she is not at work. Being on holiday recently, she found herself having 'her child' in mind: "I saw some toys and books", she says, "and I thought to myself, 'this is what he would be interested in'". She is, in fact, surprised herself by her feelings of closeness, but, at the same time, she does acknowledge that she actually wants the child to like her too. Despite her ideal of distance, she realises that "he needs to be good about the time" they spend together, as she says, and to make this happen, she has to create a situation where he is happy and comfortable. In doing that, they inevitably become close.

Trying to keep a distance is more common among nannies and au pairs who have worked for several families. This has been the case for Bonnie, whose last experience of leaving a family was upsetting. She had become very close to the two-year-old child in her care, and when she left, the child was crying and screaming, and Bonnie was very upset and sad too. She tried to make the situation better by making sure that the children would be taken care of in a good way, in a way that resembled her way of doing care, after she had left. She did this by taking very seriously the task, given to her by the parents, of introducing the new au pair to the family. In that way, under the conditions given, she tried to continue taking responsibility for the children's well-being. When now entering new families, Bonnie tries to keep a distance in order to not find herself in this difficult situation again.

Another strategy for dealing with the inevitable separation is to try to stay in contact after leaving the family. For Bea, a nanny who worked for the same family for several years, leaving the family has been a gradual process. After having worked regularly for the family, she stopped working for a while, but returned again later on. At the moment of the interview, she was looking for other jobs and just occasionally worked in the family. Leaving them step by step has meant that break-ups have been less difficult, Bea says, and as with Bonnie, she has also been responsible for introducing new nannies into the family, which has given her the possibility of – at least to some extent – ensuring that the children's future care relationships are good, even though she is not there herself.

Over the years, Bea has developed a close relationship to the whole family, but especially to the oldest daughter. When Bea decided that she was leaving the family for the first time, this child was very upset: "'Why, why do you have to work somewhere else?'", she said to Bea, and Bea continues: "And like now, when I am applying for jobs, she just 'I hope you don't get it'". Bea's relationship with the family is, in many ways, much more reciprocal than is usually the case in nanny placements. Even when she has left the family, she has still been invited to their house; she has gone on outings with the whole family, and with the children only, outside of work. However, this also makes it difficult for her to define what kind of relationship they actually have. During the interview, she poses a number of concerns: is she an employee or a family friend? Should she start charging for her visits – which, indeed, often turn into similar doings as the ones she did when she was formerly employed – or would that breach the relationship of being friends with the family? Leaving the family one step at a time has meant that she feels less worried about the well-being of the children and has enabled their close contact to remain, but it has also left her feeling unsure of her position in relation to the family.

Staying in contact is, indeed, not an option for everyone. As we saw in Chapter 3, not all parents are interested in helping their children keep in touch with their former nannies and au pairs, and while some are, relationships often fade out. This applies to nannies and au pairs too; several recognise that they will probably not be able to stay in contact since they will move away for a new job or even leave the country. While, as we have argued, the inevitable endings affect their understanding of, and relation to, the children from the start, the strategies to keep a distance are inadequate. When they find themselves in the actual care situations, distance is impossible. In the words of the nanny Fredrika:

> 'I was thinking about that, not getting too emotionally attached, but if I didn't get that attached to her, if I wouldn't feel the connection, it would somehow affect my work. So, I'd rather be a little bit heartbroken when I leave and know that I did a good job and that I had a proper relationship with her.'

Keeping a distance becomes detrimental to doing a good job as a nanny: to be good means to be in the care situation and to *engage*. To care for someone necessitates *seeing* that person, being in the moment (Mason, 1996). The emotional activities that one has to engage in to make the care situation good are not to be equated with emotions as 'states of being', such as in talk about 'love' as the new 'gold' being extracted in global care chains (Hochschild, 2002: 26). Instead, emotional activities are there regardless of emotions as states of being, and are in no way only positive in nature; on the contrary, they are often experienced as demanding and gruelling. Engaging in them does, however, affect the feelings that individuals have towards one another, as intensive engagements with other human beings do. In most cases, the care situations that the nannies and au pairs have to engage in, and the emotional doings that are required of them in these, lead to feelings of closeness, and sometimes – but not always – to feelings of 'love'. To end care situations is therefore often hurtful.

Defining one's position: part of the family, employee, or just 'lucky'

The position of nanny or au pair is often defined as being in between that of 'employee' and 'part of family', and both researchers and actors often emphasise the 'in betweenness' of her position (see, eg, Anderson, 2000; Ehrenreich and Hochschild, 2002; Búriková and Miller, 2010; Macdonald, 2010). This tension is also present in our study, both in parents' uncomfortable positionings, as we saw in Chapter 3, and in the rules and regulations for au pairs, where they are simultaneously labelled as workers and as being on 'cultural exchange' through their incorporation into a Swedish family (Anving and Eldén, 2016). This, coupled with the fact that they are directly employed by the parents, puts au pairs in a somewhat different position as compared to nannies, who, through their association with an agency, and through the fact that they do not live with the family, are – at the outset – positioned more on the employee side of the dichotomy. However, as became clear in the narratives of parents, nannies can also be seen as part of the family. Turning to the narratives of nannies and au pairs themselves, the understanding and narrating of one's own position relates to this dichotomy for both categories of workers, but it is further highly dependent on the parents' understanding of who they *should* be in the family.

Between being 'part of the family' and an employee

Labelling one's position as being 'in between' part of the family and an employee, and expressing discomfort with both positions, is as common in our interviews with nannies and au pairs as it was with parents. "You're in between, semi-family, semi-employee", as the au pair Bonnie says. However, contrary to the parents, the nannies and au pairs have less opportunity to decide for themselves and are more dependent on the parents' willingness to include or not include them in their family. The nanny Monika, who, as we saw earlier, wants to avoid being too close, works for two different families who position her very differently. One of the families treats her as "part of the outer family" circle, while in the other family, she is more like a "service provider". Keeping a distance is easier in the second family; however, it is in this family that she has developed the previously mentioned close relationship to the child. Monika's possibility of pursuing her own idea of who she is in the family is constrained by the parents' positioning. On top of that, regardless of both her own and the parents' ideas, it becomes evident in her example that a relationship to a child can sometimes turn into something else: while the point of departure for all adult actors is distance, the care situation she experiences with the child is marked by closeness.

The importance of how one is positioned by the parents is also visible in the case of the au pair Tanja. In contrast to Monika, Tanja, who is working in her first host family, is less sure of what position she herself wants to have in the family, but her host parents have a very clear idea of who she should be. Although they have not explicitly told Tanja that she is not part of the family, the way they treat her gives her no doubt: she resides in the family's cellar, and the family has told her that when her workday is over, they do not want to see her upstairs:

'Well, I do not feel like one of the family. I feel more like an employee. I feel more like one of the family than the cleaning lady, like she is more of an employee than I am, but I am not like, I am not like their extra child or anything. It is a bit more distant, or what should I say. [...] Sometimes, it is a good thing. But, sometimes, you wish you could join them more, do more things together with them.'

While she does see some advantages in this arrangement – for example, she gets more privacy, as well as a bit more control of her time – she also feels uncomfortable. She compares herself with her au pair friends who spend more time with their families and sometimes even get to go with them when they travel. Tanja wishes that the family could at least ask her if she would like to join them after hours sometimes as this would give her some evidence of them recognising that she is important to them. In the interview, Tanja negotiates her position by comparing it both with other au pairs and also with the cleaning lady, whom she regards as being even more of an employee than her: she does not live with the family and her work does not include interaction with family members. Tanja thinks that the fact that she has a close relationship to the children should give her more of a special position in the family: she relates to and cares for them, and these doings do not correspond with the position she then gets from the parents, in her view.

Contrary to Tanja, nannies and au pairs who have taken many turns in the 'nanny circle' are usually more reluctant to be positioned as 'part of the family', both because closeness to children has led to hurtful endings, as we discussed earlier, and also because this position sometimes leads to parents demanding more work (see also Anderson, 2000; Lutz, 2011; Cox, 2015). Still, their room for manoeuvre is limited: even if they themselves want to have a certain position, the parents' definition and treatment of them is determinant in the end.

Regardless of how the nannies and au pairs are positioned, almost all express discomfort: it is as if neither label fits. There seems to be a discrepancy in how one experiences doing nanny and au pair care, regardless of whether it is labelled part of the family or employee.

Downplaying the work and becoming 'part of the family'

The argument of parents using 'part of the family' to extract more work has, as argued earlier, been put forward by many scholars. Our study shows that nannies and au pairs can also make use of this labelling as a way of giving themselves and their practice value (Stubberud, 2015). Assuming the label of 'part of the family' can become a way of giving oneself agency, while simultaneously acknowledging that it results in doing more work.

Several nannies and au pairs both recognise and downplay the work they do and the responsibilities they get. The au pair Ellie, for example, who talked about her "sort of free time" in an earlier quote, continually uses diminishing expressions when describing her many tasks and working hours:

> 'But *I don't really mind because* I, I like it busy. […] I get really lazy if I don't, if I'm not busy, and then I'm like, "Okay, you're too lazy, you have to do something now". So, *I'm actually fine with it*. But I know it's, it's a bit more than others have to do, especially with the laundry. So, sometimes, it's quite a lot. […] Yeah, *I don't really mind* because that's what the mother and I also talked about in the beginning. I don't want it to be, "Okay, I have five hours today, I'm done with my five hours, I'm not gonna do anything else". Because *I'm living in that family*. If there's something more to do, *I'm completely fine, because they're also doing stuff for me* and they're really, being really generous and everything and…. So, if it's not, if it's more than five hours, *I don't really mind* it, and sometimes I'm not counting at all, so sometimes I'm not even sure. I just know that sometimes I pick up, drop off the kids and then I do the laundry, and I do some stuff for myself and all of a sudden, the day's over. And I've heard some au pairs saying, "I'm bored sometimes", and I'm never bored. I don't have time for that [laughing]. So, but it's…. But I think, at the end of this year, it's probably all in the given of five a day, five hours a day, because then I know how to do everything. In the beginning, it's just, you're really slow.' (Emphases added)

Ellie's days are busy, and her recurrent expressions "I don't mind" and "I'm fine with it" show that she is, in fact, quite aware of this too, but by using expressions like these, she appears to be more in control of the situation, and not just in the hands of the employer. Ellie gives several different explanations as to why she does not mind: she would be lazy if her days were not busy; she wants to be generous to the family as she thinks that they are being generous towards her (though it is quite unclear how this generosity is expressed); she does not want to be someone who "counts hours"; and she also speculates that it might be her fault as she is "slow" and has not learned all the chores yet. However, later on in the interview, it becomes clear that her doing of extra work for the family is not only about "not minding", but also about finding it difficult to say 'no' to tasks as she is afraid that "standing up for your free time", and to say in the evening, "'Okay now, I'm done now, I'm not gonna do this'" would disappoint the family. Instead of causing a conflict about this, something that could put her in a difficult situation, her own achievement is consequently downplayed with reference to assumptions of this being what is expected when one lives in a family.

A related strategy is to blame oneself. Ellie uses this too in the preceding quote in her talk about "maybe being too slow" in carrying out her tasks. The au pair Gloria, whom we met in the introductory example, also blames herself for the shortcomings of not being able to do everything. The stark discrepancy between Gloria's first and second interviews – praising her luck in coming to such a good family in the first one and having a much more critical and ambivalent feeling in the second – is also visible in her diary. On the one hand, Gloria describes very hard and extensive work days, and then, on the other, always finishes the description of every day with a note on how much she likes the family and loves the children:

> Today has been a tiring one. [...] I woke up to needing to start their day, which usually is not my duty. I spent the day doing laundry, which is normal, took the middle one to her afternoon tennis lesson, then took on entertaining the youngest and the oldest one and her friend. Normally, this is fine, but today I am tired. Dad came home to rest, mum is still away on business until seven pm, so dinner is my duty tonight. I just want to sleep.... I love being here for this family, they are wonderful, but occasionally I need breathing room.

The diary interview starts off by Gloria telling the interviewer that she has been "through a series of very rough days with my family", which becomes the primary focus of the interview. She feels that the workload has been heavy, that her way of caring for the children has been criticised by the parents and that she is unappreciated for the work she does. Her conclusion, however, is that her feelings are probably unfair: the parents, she says, are working so much more than her, and compared to her, their responsibilities are much more important: "they have so many other things to worry about", so maybe she is asking for too much when she wants recognition. In doing this, she is downplaying her own experience of the situation in favour of the parents'.

Nannies' and au pairs' downplaying of the work and potential problems must be understood in relation to their trying to understand their position in the family. To some extent, they do criticise their employers, some more than others, but they also see their everyday life through the employers' eyes. It is not the employers who ask too much of them, but instead they themselves who must change: do their job faster, stop complaining about not being recognised and see extra work as something that one just does when 'you are family'. Seeing themselves as family thereby becomes a way of downplaying the work part of their activity, something that paradoxically leads to them doing more work.

"I've been lucky": narrating a precarious position

Accompanying the 'I don't mind' narrative is the 'I've been lucky' narrative, which is present in almost all interviews with nannies and au pairs. Presenting the researcher with such a narrative is a way of saying that they know that the situation could have been different, that they could have been in a much worse position. The labelling of oneself as having 'luck' is done in relation to the particular family that they are working for, comparing them with other nannies' and au pairs' families, as well as families that they have worked for previously. Rumours and knowledge about others being worse off, and comparing current conditions with previous ones, work as a way of positioning one's own situation as 'at least better' than what it could have been, making maltreatment more acceptable and, again, giving the nanny or au pair a sense of being in control. The 'I've been lucky' narrative can, in part, be interpreted as a very common biographical way of presenting oneself: in general, people want to present themselves in a good light, and as being in control of their situation. However, the 'I've been lucky' stories also indicate something else, a more implicit knowledge of the nannies and au pairs about the precariousness of the nanny or au pair role as such. By talking about others' – and one's own past – problems, they point to the fact that *they know* about the inherent vulnerability of the role.

One group of au pairs – women with backgrounds in poorer non-EU countries, and especially Filipina au pairs – more often have experience of working in many families, and also more frequently talk about hardship and mistreatment (Liversage et al, 2013; Bikova, 2017).[3] This group of au pairs are in a particularly vulnerable situation at the outset: they are more dependent on their income as they often send remittances home, and au pairing is often their only way of entering Europe legally. In addition, there are underlying assumptions of race and ethnicity constructing them as especially 'good with children', efficient, hard-working and meticulous, as well as easy to exploit, both workwise and sexually (Constable, 2002). While the parents and children in our study very rarely refer to ethnicity, Filipina au pairs still occur in some instances, where they reproduce the image of this group as particularly vulnerable.

Some au pairs from this group participating in our study claim that, for them, acknowledging 'luck' is not enough: their previous experiences and reputation have necessitated their learning how to identify 'good families'. The Filipina au pair Zara, for example, has experience of very bad working conditions in previous families. One family in Denmark treated her so badly that she went to court, a case that Zara won through the help of the Danish au pair association (organised through the Danish Worker's Union). This experience has made her better at negotiating her working conditions, she says, and nowadays she even dares to say 'no' to work tasks that are not in the contract. Also, she has taken it upon herself to share her knowledge with other Filipina au pairs. Reproducing the dominant image of this group, her mission is to change the attitudes of her fellow countrywomen so that they can improve their position:

> 'I told them, "Before, I was like you, I was so shy, so timid, I could not talk to them [employer], confront them, say that I don't like this, I don't like it". Now, I read the rules, I know the rules, what it should be like. I always tell the family that it's in the contract, it's not allowed. I always tell them from the beginning […] I said to the other au pairs, "I was abused before, but now I'm strong. I used those bad experiences to become strong now".'

What differentiates Zara from most nannies and au pairs in our study is that she has come to the conclusion that to hope for 'luck' is not the solution. Instead, collective organisation is necessary, she argues, both in unions and, more informally, in supporting each other in everyday life: she herself has initiated social media groups for Filipina au pairs in Sweden, and also organises social events.

Still, formal organisation of au pairs in Sweden does not exist, and while social networks sometimes work as a medium for informing each other about rights and working conditions, and also occasionally alerts about 'bad families' (Búriková, 2015: 44), au pairs are still very isolated. In this sense, nannies are more protected due both to the fact that they are, in most cases, Swedish and less dependent on the income as compared to au pairs, and also that through their association with an agency, they have a third party to turn to in case of mistreatment (though they rarely do so, according to our interviews).[4] However, the narratives of both groups attest to the working conditions of both nannies and au pairs, within the current framework, still being highly dependent upon being lucky and coming to a 'good' family. The family's demands, attitude and definition of their position are decisive.

Conclusion: caring beyond the nanny and au pair role

What does it mean to work as a nanny or an au pair and to take care of children within the home setting of a family? To capture all aspects of nanny and au pair work, we have taken our point of departure in the nannies' and au pairs' narratives about the everyday mundane practices of care that they are engaged in. In doing so, we have been able to capture tensions between 'ideal' descriptions of what the work entails, on the one hand, and, on the other, nannies' and au pairs' more complicated and ambivalent narratives and understandings of the actual doings of care that they have to engage in and how they handle and narrate the position. We have seen how the framework for, and descriptions of, nanny and au pair work as 'easy', 'light' and limited obscure the experiences of complex emotional activities in care situations, and how the carving out of a way of being with and relating to children that works has to take place in and through negotiations of parents' expectations.

Through this, another side of the coin of the 'solving of the jigsaw puzzle of life' has emerged. While nannies and au pairs see and – sometimes – value their ability to reduce stress and enable quality time for parents, they still experience stress and conflict on their part. For them to be able to handle this is crucial: this is what makes them into 'good' nannies and au pairs. Furthermore, doing so involves not only being able to handle the care situation as such – to have knowledge about and the ability to read the specific child and the moments they share – but also being able to present solutions that are acceptable in the eyes of the parents. Not being sure of whether they are doing things right is often experienced as frustrating, not least since it is hard to label (DeVault, 1991): when instructions from parents seem clear and simple and things go wrong anyway, nannies and au pairs often search in vain for explanations. Some end up blaming themselves, some conclude that this is what it is like being 'part of the family', and surprisingly many tell us that they have come to the conclusion that nannying and au pairing was maybe not for them after all.

While au pairs and nannies are two different categories of workers, defined differently in regulations and frameworks, and differing in migratory background as well as in the level of involvement in the family, our study has shown that the similarities in the practice that they are assigned – caring for children in families – determines their situation. While ethnicity, migratory position and class background matter, there are dimensions *within the care situation as such* that are decisive for both categories of workers. This will be investigated more closely in Chapter 6. Before that, however, we turn to the last – and, indeed, most central – category of people participating in the practice of doing nanny and au pair care: children.

Children's Narratives of Nanny and Au Pair Care

Ludwig

Eleven-year-old Ludwig has just experienced the leaving of his first au pair. For almost a year, Linda, an au pair from the Philippines, had been working in the family, taking care of Ludwig and his siblings. Ludwig's memory of Linda is very bright, he really enjoyed her presence in his life and in the house, and especially her company in the afternoons: knowing that she would be there waiting for him when he got home from school made him feel safe and happy. In his draw-your-day painting, he chooses to draw that particular moment: himself and the au pair in the kitchen in the afternoon, when she is preparing his afternoon snack. Having Linda there was so "clever", he says, "You had someone there who helped you. You were not alone when you got home. It was so good that someone was there". If something was bothering him, for example, if he was upset about something when he got home from school, Ludwig felt that he could talk to her.

Ludwig also talks about all the other things Linda did in the house for him and his family: she cleaned the house; she cooked all the food; she took his smaller siblings to activities; she sometimes tucked his baby sister in, in the evening; and she also – though not very often – played with him and his siblings. He talks about one time in particular when Linda helped them build a den by the family pool. She helped them drag out mattresses, sheets and pillows, and then they all hid in there, playing a trick on his mum when she got back home from work.

'You could say that she was with us and helped us. She kind of, you could say that, she pushed us forward a bit so we could do more things, so things went faster and kind of…. So we simply could, they [parents] could work more and we could kind of, we were not home alone and…. So that was really good.'

Ludwig is both positive towards the idea of au pairing, and also expresses clearly that he had a very special relationship to Linda. In his closeness circle, he puts Linda immediately outside of the circle where he has put his family members, and closer to him than any of his other relatives, despite the fact that she was no longer working in the family at the time of the interview. He misses her, he says, especially when he gets home in the afternoon; that particular time that he felt was theirs. She was his "barnmamma" ("child-mother"), he says. He is concerned about the fact that they have not been able to stay in contact; he thinks that his mum has tried to set up a time for her to come visit again, but he himself has no means to contact her. He would really like to have an au pair again, he says, preferably Linda, or at least someone who is as good as her.

Ludwig's narrative about having an au pair is one of the most positive narratives we heard in this study: he truly enjoyed the presence of Linda in the family and thought that their bonds had been special. In fact, his particular narrative came as a surprise to the interviewer. During the research, the mother of Ludwig was interviewed too, as was one of his siblings. The mother showed quite ambivalent feelings towards the au pair and was not particularly interested in her forming close bonds with the children. Ludwig's sister's narrative was more in tune with the mother's: she had not experienced the au pair as close. Neither the sibling nor the mother missed the au pair as much as Ludwig did now that she had quit the family.

Despite this, Ludwig presents us with his narrative, full of emotion. It turns our attention to several important dimensions in the study of children and nanny and au pair care. It proves that strong, emotionally deep bonds can, indeed, develop between nannies, au pairs and children. It further shows how children are active in 'doing' the caring relationships that surround them. They are most definitely affected by the structural position that children are placed in, in this case, the current social context of care and au pairing in Sweden. The idea of au pairing as cultural exchange, the aim for gender equality on the labour market and the possibility for both Ludwig's parents to pursue demanding careers, the (somewhat unclear) rules and regulations of au pairing that, in Ludwig's case, granted the au pair a work permit, and the current political climate that makes hiring a nanny or an au pair a plausible solution to 'solving the jigsaw puzzle of life' to parents in Sweden – all of these have contributed to putting Ludwig in the situation of having Linda in his life. He has had no say in this whatsoever. Despite moves towards more inclusive and democratic modes of childrearing, as a child, Ludwig is subordinate in relation to adults, and, most importantly, of course, to his parents. It was his mother who invited the au pair into the family, and it was she who prematurely ended the contract, against Ludwig's will. However, despite this, his narrative shows the specific ways in which he carves out *his own* relationship to the au pair and how his experience of being in a care situation with the au pair has enabled this relationship to emerge. This proves the absolute necessity of including children's narratives when researching families and care. Children form positions; they act and react, use and refuse, concur and protest. They can, just as grown-ups, hold strong, unified and contradictory positions on one and the same topic. In this chapter, we present their complex narratives on nanny and au pair care.

Children and paid domestic care

Children and care is, one could argue, a thoroughly researched topic. Children are commonly talked about as *in need* of care, as recipients of different forms of caring acts, and, as such, are subject to numerous discussions, studies and theories of care. Less often are children asked about their own experiences of and reflections on their care situation. This can be explained by historical assumptions of children as incapable of narrating their own lives that, notwithstanding challenges from childhood scholars (Prout, 2005; Christensen and James, 2008; Sandin, 2012; Davies, 2015), still endure. Despite this, research that has included and analysed children's views on care has pointed towards the reciprocal character of the practice. Care is not merely 'done' to children; children are 'active co-participants in care and co-constructors of family life' who, like adults, 'make sense of the rules which guide caring behaviour and negotiate them in relation to particular contexts and situations' (Brannen et al, 2000: 212; Eldén, 2016). They are part of the care situation that is created by surrounding structural frameworks, but within this situation, they act, react and form, or reject, practices and relationships.

The care situation involving children being taken care of by nannies and au pairs has been theorised about in the literature on global care chains, and as we argued in Chapter 2. The main argument has been that children being taken care of by nannies and au pairs are at the 'winner' end of the global care chain (Hochschild, 2002). The literature points towards the risk of children starting to treat people as means rather than ends in themselves, and of the practice of hiring nannies fostering undemocratic citizens (Tronto, 2002: 40). However, empirical studies taking their point of departure in children's own narratives also attest to children's experiences of close caring relations with maids and nannies: children talk about the domestic worker as being a 'second mother' (Spyro, 2009: 162), and children's and nannies' mutual engagement in the everyday doings of care is seen as a relationship-building enterprise (Sourolová, 2013: 154). In common with these children-centred studies, our aim in this study has been to capture children's narratives of the relational doings of care in their everyday lives.

Nineteen children, aged between five and 14 years old, were interviewed. We met with nine girls and ten boys,[1] and as with the parents in our study, several of the children's families could be characterised as financially well off. Many of the houses and apartments that we visited when doing the interviews were large and situated in affluent neighbourhoods; several children showed us new computers and other expensive equipment in their rooms, and many told us about a lifestyle where trips abroad several times a year are common. However, we also met with children who live in average middle-class families. Common to all children in this study is that both their parents work full time (or more). The children have had different experiences of having nannies and au pairs: some have had nannies or au pairs for as long as they could remember, while some have had just one. Taken altogether, they told us about experiences of around 80 nannies and au pairs. The children do not seem to differentiate a lot between the two categories: the narratives of nanny care and au pair care are strikingly similar in our interviews with children, and the term 'barnflicka' ('nanny') was often used in talking about both nannies and au pairs.

In the following, we discuss, first, the children's understandings of and reflections upon their parents' decision to hire nannies and au pairs, as well as their ideas of what this has brought to family life. Second, we turn to the children's narratives of the nannies' and au pairs' presence in their everyday lives: what do they *do* according to the children? This doing is intertwined with how the child perceives the relationship between him/herself and the nanny or the au pair: who is she to the child? Finally, the chapter ends with narratives of beginnings and endings, of children talking about getting to know and saying goodbye to nannies and au pairs, an experience often charged with strong emotions.

"Mum and dad can work, but we're never alone": understanding the presence of nannies and au pairs

In the children's narratives, the most common understanding of why the family has employed a nanny or an au pair has to do with the parents' working situation: since the parents have to work, and since their work is so demanding, someone else needs to be there to take care of us, the children say. A common way of talking about the parents' working situation is as a non-negotiable fact – as the way things are. When 14-year-old Jonathan talks about the reasons that his family has employed over ten nannies and au pairs over the years, he says "Many people might think that if you have a nanny, then you are less connected with your family, that you get, like, get to see your parents less. But the reason we had nannies was that we couldn't see them anyway because they worked too much". For Jonathan, it is obvious that he and his brother need to be taken care of by someone, and since his parents are not there, their presence has to be substituted by someone else; otherwise, they would be on their own, which is not an option. Neither is it an option for Jonathan that the parents could work less.

When reflecting on the parents' demanding work situation, children often express themselves in ambiguous ways. On the one hand, they see the good things that the parents' work brings to the family, most importantly, more money and, through that, the possibility of living in a nice house, buying nice things and having more opportunities to go on vacation. However, simultaneously, this is also a cause for critical reflections. In replying to questions of what is good and not so good about her family, ten-year-old Camilla talks about and negotiates the parents' working situation:

Researcher:	'Is there something that is not so good about your family?'
Camilla:	'That mum and dad work so much; that is sort of why we have this [the nannies] because if we didn't have it like this, then we would be, if we went to – when I went to after-school care, I would be picked up at five, or half past five maybe…. […] But it's good too because we go on vacation much more often.'
Researcher:	'Oh, I see. So, you think that is something you can do because they work so much, or…?'
Camilla:	'Mm. So that's what you kind of think about, that they're doing it for us and not for….'

When talking about their parents' heavy workload, children acknowledge the negative consequences that this has for them and their siblings. At the same time, the critical aspects are nuanced by the identification of the good things that this brings to the family. Camilla's account of her trying to think about "this" – which, in her thinking, refers to the situation emerging as a consequence of their decision, of which the nannies and au pairs are part – as something they "do for us" indicates complex negotiations on her part: she is trying to understand the parents' decision, although she experiences the consequences as being in some ways negative. As we will see later on, Camilla has very ambivalent feelings towards the presence of nannies and au pairs in her everyday life.

Apart from taking in and understanding – and also being critical towards – the parents' working situation as the cause of the decision to hire nannies and au pairs, the children also see and talk about other potential reasons for the presence of nannies and au pairs in their lives. This is connected to ideas about the consequences of the nanny being there, of what good and bad things it brings to them and to family life in general. Several children talk about the nanny and the au pair as a person who enhances family life and makes it better. While the children (unlike the parents) do not use the terminology of 'solving the jigsaw puzzle of life', they do see and talk about the nannies' and au pairs' doings in everyday life as helping the family: they "push" us forward so "we could do more things", and do them "faster", as Ludwig expressed it. Having someone else helping out with different chores is seen as helping both the parents and the children themselves so that they can do more things that they enjoy. Fiona (11 years old) talks about how the au pair's taking care of her younger siblings relieves her from care work since they have "someone else to go to" when they need something. Several children mention that nannies and au pairs "clean up after you when you have played with stuff", pointing out that this is really good since the children themselves do "not really like to", or are "not so good at" it. The children's thoughts on the 'doings' of nannies and au pairs are complex, as we will discuss in more detail later, but it is evident that there are aspects of this doing that the children see as relieving them from 'boring duties' and thereby enhancing the quality of life for themselves and for the whole family.

In addition, some children also see and talk about how the au pairs' ability to teach them English has meant that they have had an advantage in comparison to their classmates in school. However, most also talk about this as being difficult, as seen in the interview with 11-year-old Theo:

Researcher: 'So, did they speak English all of them, the au pairs and the nannies?'

Theo: 'Yes, although my mum....[...] Dad's friends, their children, they knew English, and my brother and I didn't, when we were younger.... [...] And then they [parents] decided that they wanted us to learn English, although I didn't want to, and then kind of....'

Researcher: 'How old were you then?'

Theo: 'Four, maybe. And I really didn't want to learn, but then they hired English-speaking au pairs, and then we just had to learn.'

Researcher: 'How was that? Was it hard in the beginning?'

Theo: 'Yes it was because I only knew like "hello" and ... [...] yes, those kinds of words, so it was really, really hard.'

Theo does mention later on that this has made him "second best" at English in school, which he appreciates, but he clearly still remembers the hardship of having to deal with this in his everyday life. Again, as is the case with the arguments about parents' heavy workload, the children express both understandings of, and critical reflections towards, the parents' wish for them to learn English from the au pair.

On some occasions in our interviews, children openly questioned the parents' decision to have a nanny or an au pair. Interestingly, this position might be expressed in addition to acknowledging the good things that a nanny or an au pair brings to the family. Emily (nine years old), for example, who has had more than four au pairs involved in her everyday care over the years, says that the au pair is necessary since she reduces the stress in the family, for the parents and for herself, but simultaneously, she questions the whole idea of having an au pair. When the interviewer asks her what she likes about having an au pair, she pauses for quite some time and then replies: "One thing, I think that, when you get an au pair, why do you even have children, if you cannot take care of them and get an au pair instead? So, that's one thing I've been thinking about".

Contrary to the parents' narratives, which express a more thoroughly positive attitude towards the 'gains' of hiring nannies and au pairs, the children's reports are more ambiguous. On the one hand, the children express and name the same 'gains' as the parents. They see the need for (and some positive effects of) the parents' heavy workload, including the mothers' (none of the children distinguish between their parents' genders when talking about their working situation). They see the advantage in not having to stay long hours at daycare or after-school activities, and they value the relief in care work that both the parents and themselves experience with a nanny or an au pair present. They also see the advantageous position that they have gained in comparison to other children through au pairs having taught them a different language. On the other hand, and simultaneously, children do express criticism and concern. Although they are often aware of the wishes and aims of the parents, these do not always correspond with the wishes and wants of the children, or with their actual experience of being in a care situation with a nanny or an au pair. Interestingly, in her study of children at the other end of the care chain – Filipino children left behind by migrating domestic workers – Parreñas (2001) encountered similar attitudes and ambiguous understandings: while the children reported on the emotional hardship of being separated from their parents, they also saw the 'care' within their mothers' decision to migrate for the benefit of the whole family. The children in our study, while being on the 'winning end' of the care chain, report in analogous terms: while in no way being as estranged from their parents, they also have to make sense of parental absence in their everyday life.

"She's just there, always": nannies and au pairs in children's everyday lives

Regardless of how the parents frame the nanny/au pair care – why she is there, what they expect of her or how much, and how they try to orchestrate the caring situation through lists or ideas of 'qualitative activities' – it is still done, enacted and experienced in practices involving primarily the nanny and the child. As was shown in Chapter 4, parents are indirectly present in these care situations, both in the minds of the nannies and au pairs, and in the different ways in which they set the frame for the practice. However, regardless of this, the nanny or the au pair finds herself in situations where she and the child are the primary actors. Nannies' and au pairs' ways of dealing with the parents' expectations, while simultaneously having their own situationally created 'knowledge' of how the care situation should be dealt with, came through as critical. Now we turn our attention to the other actors' descriptions of experiences of this caring situation: the children's narratives of everyday 'doings', and how the children perceive the presence of nannies and au pairs in their everyday lives – what she *does* according to the children. This, in turn, is intertwined with how the children perceive the relationship between themselves and the nanny/au pair. Who is she to the child?

A constant presence

All our interviews with children testify to the fact that they see and acknowledge the things that nannies and au pairs do in their everyday lives, as in the introductory example of Ludwig: Linda's doings are seen as diverse and all encompassing; she is doing almost everything – from cleaning the house to tucking in his baby sister. That the children's interviews entail these descriptions are, one could argue, not surprising given our methods: we ask about and encourage children to talk about and reflect upon their everyday lives. However, the draw-your-day exercise does not ask about nannies and au pairs per se, but about the child's everyday life. Thus, it becomes obvious that the nannies and au pairs are very present in the children's everyday lives.

So, what are nannies and au pairs doing, then, according to the children? In some children's narratives, the presence is vast, and the nannies and au pairs are so taken for granted that it is not even reflected upon: she is just always there, and she does everything. Six-year-old Annelie, for example, has had several au pairs and nannies over the years, and the current au pair, Amanda, is ever present in Annelie's telling about her day. The au pair wakes her up in the morning and prepares and serves breakfast: "Look", Annelie says, and points to the drawing, "that's Amanda. She has already put breakfast on the table when you get down to the kitchen. What a luxury, isn't it!?". The au pair knows what Annelie's favourite food is, and after breakfast, she drives Annelie to school. She picks her up again in the afternoon, she takes her to activities, she prepares dinner for the whole family and she does the dishes afterwards, and sometimes she puts Annelie and her siblings to bed. On top of that, she does all of the laundry, Annelie tells us, and proudly states that she herself helps out with this.

Other children talk about a more limited or divided presence, where the nanny or the au pair is doing more designated tasks. This is more often the case when the child has a RUT nanny taking care of him/her, which is not surprising since the nanny is not living together with the family and usually only spends a couple of afternoons a week with the child.

Special doings

Certain activities that nannies and au pairs do – or do not do – with children stand out in the narratives and are described in terms and with expressions that make them seem more important to the child. These activities can sometimes be easily categorised as chores, such as baking or tucking in at night, but they can also be more vaguely described as doings and beings, such as in expressions like "someone to talk to", "someone who knows what I like" or who is "there for me".

Some activities are mentioned in especially pleasurable terms, and these are often activities that the children talk about as things they did *together* with the nanny. As mentioned earlier, Annelie is very proud of the fact that she is helping the nanny to do laundry, which reflects previous studies of children's pride in having caring competence (Christensen, 2002; Eldén, 2016). Thinking back at the different nannies that he has had over the years, 12-year-old Ivan remembers one particular girl that he liked and how they used to bake different things together: "She really liked to bake, that's one of the things I remember about her. We used to make.… What's it called? Cookies. We made, like, cupcakes and chocolate chip cookies … and I really enjoyed that too".

Descriptions in the children's narratives of the pleasures of baking (and eating) cookies together can be compared with those in the narratives of both the parents and the nannies/au pairs: the parents assigning baking as an activity that they happily approve of when orchestrating the quality time of the nanny and the child, and the nannies talking about trying to fulfil this wish – sometimes gladly but sometimes with more negative feelings. From the perspectives of the children, baking cookies becomes an activity that stands out as extra and special, and as something that the nannies seem to be doing both for their own pleasure and for the child's, as something done especially *for them*.

Likewise, children's talk of nannies and au pairs' engaging in play comes out as important. As childhood scholars have argued, play is inherently integral to children's social worlds (Schwartzman, 1978) and a key medium through which children relate to friends (Wyness, 2006; James and James, 2008; Corsaro, 2015). In the narratives of children in our study, play becomes a significant sign of how the child relates to the nanny or the au pair: reports about play signal her being there for them, knowing what they like and engaging in their world and pleasures. However, the topic of play often occurs in talk about what the nanny or au pair *does not* normally do. In the introductory example with Ludwig, the building of a den was mentioned as a rare occasion, as a treasured memory. Similarly, when asked about what she does together with her au pair Amanda, Annelie starts talking about a special occasion when Amanda's sister was visiting:

Annelie: 'When her sister was here, then we played together, then me and my brother, I was sitting on Amanda's sister's back, and my brother was sitting on the back of Amanda, and we played that we were horses,

	and we were kind of fighting, butting each other [laughs]. Like this!' [Shows the researcher what they did, laughs.]
Researcher:	'How crazy [laughs]! Do you usually play horses with Amanda?'
Annelie:	'But it was really just that one time, now that she [the sister] was here. We do not usually play together.'

Playing together is a theme that often comes up, as in Ludwig's and Annelie's narratives, in accounts about occasions when play *did* happen, as stories of the exception to the way things normally are. Interestingly, the children's narratives about the scarce prevalence of play in their everyday interactions with nannies and au pairs stands in contrast to parents' expectations of the nanny's/au pair's *engagement* with the child through, for example, play. A telling moment occurs in one of our interviews with a mother, when her five-year-old child shows up and the parent interrupts the interview to ask her child: "What do you do with Nadja? What do you do when you play?". The child replies, "If she has already finished making dinner, then we can do a jigsaw puzzle". The children's narratives of lack of play correspond better with the nannies' and au pairs' narratives than with the parents' regarding what is taking place in the care situation: there are plenty of caring chores that nannies and au pairs have to attend to before or instead of playing with the children. The view of the possibility for the nanny or au pair to 'choose' to do everything in the afternoon, expressed, for example, by the mother Nelly in Chapter 3 (walk the dogs, prepare food, be with the children, take care of the laundry), comes out as rather unrealistic not only in the narratives of nannies and au pairs, but also in those of children. However, when play does happen, it is portrayed as an occasion of significance when the child feels connection and closeness: when a nanny or au pair is doing things that the children like, she enhances their time together and proves to the child that she knows what he/she enjoys in life – and this, the children really like.

The children's appreciation of – or dissatisfaction with – the nannies' and au pairs' knowledge about them also comes out clearly in talk about food practices. As DeVault (1991) has argued, preparing food for someone else is a complex and emotionally imbued activity of caring, and in these families, it is an activity often delegated to nannies and au pairs. It is also a significant moment of time that is shared between nannies, au pairs and children: the preparing of an afternoon snack or dinner, and sometimes also the time for sitting down and sharing a meal. The *knowing* of a nanny or au pair of likes and dislikes comes out as important, for example, as in

Theo's strongest positive memory of his former au pair: every week after football practice, she made him pasta carbonara. The au pair knew that this was Theo's favourite food, and by preparing this for him, she made the moment of coming home from his football practice into a special moment where she showed him that she *knew* him and appreciated him.

Talk about food practices can also serve as a hub for negotiating more ambiguous relationships with a nanny or an au pair. In the interview with Nomie, a nine-year-old girl whose au pair, Nicky, had recently left the family at the time of the interview, food is a reoccurring theme. Nomie did not like the ethnic character of the food that the au pair cooked for the family, she tells us. Also, she did not like the afternoon snack that the au pair prepared. In her draw-your-day picture (see Figure 2), Nomie chooses to draw the au pair standing at the counter in the kitchen, cutting vegetables:

Nomie:	'She always cut it, like [laughs]....'
Researcher:	'Yes, you said she was cutting vegetables, yeah. Did she always do that?'
Nomie:	'Yes, every day.'
Researcher:	'Every day.'
Nomie:	'And then you were not allowed to eat fruit when you got home from school.'
Researcher:	'No?'
Nomie:	'Then we had to eat vegetables.'
Researcher:	'Oh, I see. How did you like that?'
Nomie:	'I didn't like that, at all. I don't like vegetables that much.'

For Nomie, this image of the au pair cutting vegetables was one of the strongest in her memory of the au pair, and it was a negative one. What Nomie did not know was that the decision to serve vegetables as an afternoon snack was not Nicky's, but the mother's, something that was told to us by both the mother and the au pair in their interviews. The au pair felt obliged to do as the mother said. We do not know if it would have made any difference to Nomie had she known that the vegetable decision was not the au pair's, but it is obvious that the au pair's doing of this simple care chore *did* affect Nomie and the au pair's relationship. Reflecting on the fact that the au pair has left the family, food again plays an important part:

Nomie:	'It was a bit sad [that she quit], maybe, but I was also kind of happy in a way because now we would get

Figure 2: Nomie's 'draw-your-day' picture

different food, like meatballs and macaroni, like we had before. Yeah, but it was a bit sad too. And, like, not too long ago, we did some homemade sweets, and then mum took a picture, and we sent it to Nicky so she would remember, kind of.'

Researcher: 'Right. Because there was, like, some stuff that you liked to do together with her then?'

Nomie: 'Yes.'

Nomie and Nicky did have some space in their relationship for more positive interactions, and some of these were also connected to food practices. The making of homemade sweets, something that was introduced to the family by the au pair, was a positive memory for Nomie. Also, Nomie told about how she used to sneak into Nicky's room, despite the stated rules that this was the area where she should have her privacy. Nicky did not mind her being there, and she sometimes did Nomie's nails, which Nomie really liked. Nicky kept boxes of sweets in her room, Nomie tells us, and she offered them to Nomie. The au pair's own space seems to have become a place for pleasure for the two of them, where the food rules of the family could also be disregarded.

Nomie's overall ambivalent feelings towards the au pair are closely connected to her experience of her everyday doings of care – some things she did not like and some things were good – and, altogether, this makes Nomie reluctant to have a precise opinion on au pairs, both in relation to this specific au pair and also towards the general idea of having an au pair or a nanny:

Researcher: 'Would you like to have more contact with Nicky?'

Nomie: 'No.'

Researcher: 'Not really, no. Would you like to have another au pair some time again?'

Nomie: 'No.'

Researcher: 'No.... [...] Is it better to be without?'

Nomie: 'Yes, I think so. Or not always; sometimes, it's fun sometimes. Sometimes you don't want to and sometimes you want to.'

When talking about the everyday care doings of the au pair, Nomie is also talking about the relationship she has formed with the au pair. The au pair's presence is intertwined with her doings: her being in the kitchen performing the chore of cutting vegetables; her initiation of new food tastes and practices in the family; her not knowing (in the eyes of

Nomie) and/or disregarding of Nomie's likes and dislikes of food; and her occasional opening up of her room to engage in activities and the sharing of pleasures – all of these doings in the care situation become the foundation upon which Nomie builds her relationship with the au pair. When she expresses her reluctance and ambivalence towards the au pair, she does so in relation to all these doings.

Another caring activity that stands out as especially defining when the children talk about their experiences of nanny and au pair care is 'tucking in at night'. While some of the younger children whose parents work late nights describe the 'tucking in' as a quite taken-for-granted thing that the nanny or au pair just does, the older children, and especially the children who have had several nannies and au pairs, use 'tucking in' as an indicator to describe to the interviewer how close or distant a current or former nanny or au pair is or was. Camilla, for example, who is very unhappy with the current au pair, and who is also very critical in general towards the many nannies and au pairs that she has had in her life, says emphatically that she is the one deciding who gets to tuck her in:

Researcher:	'So, tucking in at night, you said, is it mum and dad? It's not your au pair who does that, or...?'
Camilla:	'No.'
Researcher:	'No. Was it the same when you had Carla [former nanny]?'
Camilla:	'No, she could tuck me in at night, like, be with me.'
Researcher:	'Carla could tuck you in at night?'
Camilla:	'Mm.'
Researcher:	'Is it you who decides who gets to tuck you in, or...?'
Camilla:	'Yes.'
Researcher:	'Ok. Has there been someone else besides Carla who has tucked you in or...?'
Camilla:	'No.'
Researcher:	'Just Carla.'
Camilla:	'Mm. And grandma, of course.'

Camilla is using different strategies to take control of a situation that she is not happy about, and one of them is granting or refusing the nannies and au pairs access to situations and activities that she experience as 'close'. While she cannot resist the overall presence of the nannies and au pairs, and while some caring activities that they do are out of her control, others, like the tucking in at night, Camilla can resist. Studies of relationships between employer mothers and carers have shown that bedtime activities, such as tucking in or reading a bedtime story, are often 'kept' by parents to preserve their role as the 'most important' carer (Chan, 2005; O'Connell, 2010). Our interviews with children show that these moments serve as important markers of closeness for them too, but the granting of nanny or au pair access to this space is less dependent on her position as 'not parent' and more dependent on the child's feeling of closeness in and through the specific relationship they form.

'Being there'

Another doing, perhaps not immediately thought of as a doing of care, that emerges in the children's narratives is that nannies and au pairs are people you *talk to*. Some children talk about how they confide in their nannies and au pairs, and tell them things that they do not want others to know about. However, children also talk appreciatively about the general everyday interaction, verbal and non-verbal, that is made possible just by the fact that the nanny or au pair *is there*, together with them.

As we saw in the introductory example, the au pair's presence gave Ludwig a feeling of being safe, of knowing that she was there for him. He returns to one specific moment in his daily schedule several times during the interview: the au pair Linda standing in the kitchen preparing afternoon snacks when he and his siblings get home from school. This particular moment stands out in his narrative – and, indeed, in many other children's narratives as well – as an important time during the day, when he and the au pair talked, when they got to know each other better and when he could share both good and bad things with her:

Researcher: [About the drawing] 'So that's you, then, on your way home from school. So, what do you do then, when you get home from school?'

Ludwig: 'Then I usually, when I get home, I usually do my homework, but first when I get home, I have an afternoon snack. I usually have yoghurt and, and then I used to talk to Linda. She learned a lot of Swedish from me.' [Ludwig draws himself and the au pair together in the kitchen. He is sitting at the table, smiling; she is walking from the fridge, towards him, carrying a tin of yoghurt. She is also smiling.]

Researcher: 'So, what did you talk about?'

Ludwig: 'Like, everything. Nothing special, really. It's, like, it just comes. For some reason or another, you just start talking about something.'

Researcher:	'Was she good to talk to?'
Ludwig:	'Yes. [...] You felt like you could talk to her, kind of. She was there and she understood. She, like, helped out.'
Researcher:	'That's good.'
Ludwig:	'She was, like, she understood things really well. It was not like she didn't understand things; she really understood the situation well and, like, talked to you.'

Now that Linda has quit the family, Ludwig really misses her being there in the kitchen when he gets home from school. He sometimes forgets that she is not there. "Some days you think she will just be there, kind of", he says, and he gets sad when he comes home to find the house empty. Her 'being there' is an important part of the care situation that Ludwig experiences with his au pair, and it is closely intertwined with the more practical everyday doings that are part of her assigned chore: to serve him an afternoon snack.

In Camilla's narrative, the 'talk to' and 'being there' dimensions are used in similar ways to the way she used the 'tucking-in-at-night' practice: to distinguish between her relationships with different nannies. She could talk to the favourite nanny, Carla, if she was sad, she says, but she would never talk to any one of the others that have been taking care of her. Since she has stayed in contact with Carla, she also continuously confides in her over the phone, and also when they occasionally meet. In contrast to how she experienced the presence of Carla, the presence of the current au pair feels like an intrusion into Camilla's privacy: "There is always someone at home", she says several times in her interview, "that's kind of hard, then you cannot really have privacy", "I can, like, never be home alone and have friends over without someone interfering in what we do". Camilla's description of the nanny/au pair presence stands in stark contrast to Ludwig's: the same things that he appreciates are the things that she really cannot stand about having a nanny or an au pair. Camilla is, however, not negative towards *all* nanny presence; on the contrary, she says that she would be more than happy to have a larger presence of Carla in her everyday life as her presence is not at all intrusive, but rather appreciated and wanted.

Several children also engage in reflecting on the different ways in which nannies and au pairs are present in their lives. Twelve-year-old Karl, who has had many au pairs taking care of him over the years, compares the ways in which the au pairs "did their work" in his family: while some "did a lot" together with him and his siblings, others seemed to be doing just the bare minimum:

'There was this nanny that we had, like maybe three, four nannies ago, and like, she was here, and she was really nice and all [...] but she was like, "Yes, I'm going to go Skype with my family now", and then she was down there [in her room] for a really long time, and then she came up to make some food, and then she went downstairs again. Or she was sitting together with us [him and his sibling] when we ate our food, but then she was most of her time downstairs, kind of, and then, well then you didn't talk to her that much. But our latest nanny [...] she talked a lot to us because she did a lot of stuff together with us and came up with things we could do, like biking together.... She did a lot together with us.'

The au pair's way of just doing the bare minimum felt wrong to Karl: while he did see that she performed all the tasks that she had been asked to do by the parents, something was still missing in comparison to other au pairs he had had. Similarly, Ivan also reflects a lot upon the different ways in which all the au pairs he has had (more than ten) have been present. He is especially concerned about negotiating the 'doing' and the 'being there' in trying to understand the current situation, where the au pairs have been replaced by a 'maid'. During the interview, it becomes apparent that he is not really sure himself of what the difference is because they are, indeed, doing very similar things. The maid Josephine is living in the house, in the same space as the au pairs formerly occupied; she is almost always at home when he gets home from school; she makes him an afternoon snack; she makes dinner for the whole family; she takes care of the pets, cleans the house and does all the grocery shopping; and she takes care of him when he is ill. Ivan thinks she is 'really nice', and when doing his closeness–circle exercise, he discusses whether he should include Josephine or not. If he still had the au pairs, he would put them "just next to me", he says, in the same circle as his parents, siblings and best friend, but he is unsure of whether he should include Josephine. In the end, he decides not to:

Ivan:	'I usually do not talk to Josephine about these kinds of things.'
Researcher:	'No.'
Ivan:	'No, because she.... I, I don't really know why, but she is not really like.... I don't know her as well as I knew the others who were here.'

The same reason – that he does "not talk to Josephine" in the same way as he talked to the former au pairs – makes him refrain from calling her 'part of the family', while he would include the au pairs in the family. The au pairs were "with us most of the time", they were more "social", watched TV with the family and joined them for vacations, he says. This makes him reflect further: given that he is now older and actually does not need as much help with practical caring chores anymore, it really should be the other way around as it would make more sense if Josephine were doing more of the social part of caring, of being more with him, "because I don't really need someone to take care of me anymore".

The similarities between what the maid actually *does* in the family and what the au pairs did seem to make it difficult for him to say *how* and *why* she is different. He talks about her *not being there in the same way* as the others, as not being 'with us'. While there are some activities that the maid does not do and some of the au pairs did more often, this idea of being 'with us' seems to be more of an attitude towards who she is to the family. Ivan has been told by his parents that she is a maid and not an au pair. However, the enterprise of making this distinction work with his own experiences of having her in the house, taking care of him, is quite hard. The reason for this is that the 'care doings' of Josephine are hard to separate from the 'being there' dimensions of care. These, in turn, make Josephine's position into something more than the role of maid, even though, as a maid, she is explicitly defined as someone who is further away from the family.

The children's talk about the everyday care doings of nannies and au pairs shows that for doings to be good, they have to entail something more than just carrying out the caring chore. A good nanny and au pair is someone who shows the child that he or she is special through knowing what the child likes, through knowing when to 'be there' and when to withdraw and give the child privacy, and through 'being there' and being available and not withdrawing into her room when the chores are finished. In fact, the 'doing' of care chores seems to be difficult to separate from the qualities of 'being there'. The doing of care, as such, seems to create an expectation on the part of the children of a 'being there', of something that goes beyond the mere chores.

Negotiating closeness

Relationships are formed in the midst of everyday care doings. When the children negotiate the presence of the nannies and au pairs, their closeness and distance, the use of family terminology is common. In addition, the 'nanny circle' of enterings, exitings and re-enterings affects the ways in which children narrate and engage with nannies and au pairs.

Relating to a nanny or an au pair and negotiating family

While the question of whether or not the nanny or au pair is part of the family was, indeed, one of the questions we asked in the interviews, quite a few of the children brought this up spontaneously. Calling a nanny or an au pair "an extra parent", talking about her as being "like a bigger sister" or, on the contrary, excluding her from the family was a way of signalling closeness, likeness and distance. Again, significant in these family negotiations are reflections upon the *doings* and *beings* of the nannies and au pairs within the family and in the family home. The activities she engaged in, the everyday caring activities and the fact that she is doing them in the family home seems to make her 'family-like'. Whether she is included or not depends on *the ways* in which she carries out caring chores. Karl, for example, while using expressions such as "extra parent" during his interview, is still not entirely sure of whether he thinks that his au pairs have been part of the family:

Researcher:	'When you think about your au pairs, do you think that they have been like part of your family? Would you describe them as part of your family?'
Karl:	'No, I don't think I would describe them as family, but it was almost like they became family because they were in the house, and they – you did many things together with them in your everyday life and you spent quite a lot of time together with them. [...]'
Researcher:	'Or did it feel more like they worked here or...?'
Karl:	'It felt more like they were here, and like.... I didn't really feel like they worked here.'
Researcher:	'No, I understand, but that you were a bit family-like.'
Karl:	'Yes, a little.'
Researcher:	'But maybe that was different between different au pairs?'
Karl:	'Yes, it was like Kim, she, she was kind of, with her, that feeling was more there. She was a little bit like family, while others, some you didn't like that much and some were.... Like the one who was from Germany, she did things quite – like, she was in her room a lot, and she did the food really quickly and tried to, like, she was not together with us, and then it didn't feel at all as much that she was part of the family. It almost didn't feel like that at all.'

Researcher: 'No.'
Karl: 'Then it felt like she was just working here.'

The fact that the au pairs are spending a lot of time together with the children in the house makes them like family, according to Karl. However, the way in which they spend their time with him is important: just doing what they are supposed to do is not enough. The good au pair, then, like Kim, is part of the family because she is doing more than her designated duties.

The location of the au pair – that she spends most of her days in the house, doing house-related things – is also crucial to the children in negotiating the au pair's or nanny's 'family position'. The fact that she is in the house together with them, and sometimes also lives in the house, seems to make it necessary to reflect upon her status as 'part of family', although not everyone comes to the conclusion that this grants her the status as 'part of the family'.

The negotiations of whether or not to include the nanny or the au pair in the family are complex, as they are for the parents, as we saw in Chapter 3. Many children feel unsure: it feels wrong to include them, but also wrong not to include them. She is "a little bit part of the family", as eight-year-old Harry says, or part of the family "but only for a little while", as five-year-old Malin puts it. While having its problems, family terminology still seems to be the chosen and available way for the children to frame nannies and au pairs, and in contrast to the parents, very few children talk about nannies and au pairs as employed (Murray, 1998). When they do, as Karl did earlier, it is a way of describing a 'not so good' nanny or au pair, someone who did not do her job well. What seems to motivate the use and negotiations of nannies and au pairs in terms of 'family' is, again, their doings and beings: her place in the home, her doing of caring chores and her being in the everyday life of the child. The care situation they have to, and do, engage in together seems to make reflections through family terminology inevitable.

"Why did you come here in the first place?": forming bonds and saying goodbye

Nannies and au pairs have come and gone in the lives of the children in our study. In contrast to some other national contexts, the engagement of nannies and au pairs is, in most cases, short in Sweden. A few of the children in our study have experiences of having the same nanny or au pair involved in their lives for as long as three years, but the most common time period for which a nanny or an au pair stays with the family is one year. This means that all the children we met have experienced at least one ending of a nanny or an au pair relationship; most have experienced several, and some even as many as ten. A few cannot remember all the au pairs and nannies that they have had taking care of them over the years as they were often very small when the first one arrived. All children have also, of course, experienced the entering of a nanny or an au pair into the family, and most have furthermore experienced the entry of a new nanny or au pair after having said goodbye to an old one.

The narratives of the forming of bonds and saying goodbye are the most emotionally engaging parts of our interviews. On some occasions, the children's accounts are still full of emotions; sometimes their expressions are more factual, but also in these latter cases, the children often talk explicitly about emotions, of having learned to control and handle their feelings over the years. The children's narratives tell about a continuous circular movement in their lives, what we have called a 'nanny circle': of getting to know someone, of saying goodbye, then getting to know someone new who is entering into the same role as the former nanny or au pair, and then eventually saying goodbye again.

Entering and exiting the nanny circle...

Narratives about first meetings with nannies and au pairs often entail words and expressions of being "difficult" or "a bit scary", or of the child being nervous; feelings that are then described as eventually disappearing as the child gets used to the nanny or au pair. In Ludwig's description of the first encounter with Linda, the insecurity in the beginning is soon transformed into something more positive. He talks about her first visit, how he and his sister had baked a cake to welcome her, and how she told them about herself, but since he did not speak English, he could not understand what she said. Then, a week later, she moved in and started working in the family. "It was difficult to talk to her" in the beginning, Ludwig says, but soon they became close friends. Having someone new in the house, sometimes even someone who speaks a different language, and, in addition, someone whom you spend time alone with, is described as a challenge. Getting to know the person, getting used to her being there, takes some time, according to the children.

The children's accounts of the times when nannies and au pairs have left the family are full of emotions, mostly negative ones, of being sad, crying and not really understanding why she had to leave. For eight-year-old Sigvard, who has had more than five nannies and au pairs over the years, all goodbyes have been difficult:

Sigvard:	'I miss all my au pairs and nannies.'
Researcher:	'Have you had many au pairs?'
Sigvard:	'I have had both au pairs and nannies. [...] It is hard to get to know them at first, and changing from one to another is hard because I liked the old ones so much.'
Researcher:	'Does that make you sad then?'
Sigvard:	'Yes, I used to cry all the time.'

While for Sigvard, all nannies and au pairs have been hard to say goodbye to, other children discriminate between different nannies. Jonathan remembers the goodbyes from his childhood as "a bit sad when they left", and "if there was someone I had become good friends with", it was hard, he says. Karl remembers some endings as hard, but also some others as a relief:

'It was ... or it was rather good for me and my little brother, or I thought it was a relief. Then, of course, it wasn't very good for my parents because then they had to pick us up at daycare and stuff [in the time between two nannies/au pairs], but it was good when they [the au pairs], when you thought that they were not really good, then it was a relief when they left.'

For Emily, a particular incident when a former au pair left the family stands out in her memory. The au pair Yrsa wanted to earn some extra money, and the host mother helped her to get a weekend job:

Emily:	'Why did Yrsa just, I mean, mum had helped her get another job, and then Yrsa thought it was more fun there, and she didn't want to keep on working with us. [...] She just quit, she just walked away.'
Researcher:	'Oh. How did that feel?'
Emily:	'Not good really. [...]'
Researcher:	'Did she tell you and your siblings about it...?'
Emily:	'No.'
Researcher:	'Yeah, that must have felt a bit strange.'
Emily:	'Mm.'
Researcher:	'When you just disappear like that.'
Emily:	'Yes.'

For Emily, Yrsa's leaving the family for another job seems like a betrayal. The way in which Emily talks about Yrsa finding the other job "more fun" than "working with us", that is, taking care of Emily and her siblings, and, in addition, that she "just walked away" without saying goodbye to the children, exposes the whole experience as full of negative emotions.

…and then entering again

Emily's experience of the entering and leaving of nannies – and, as we just saw, some of the leavings being quite abrupt – has made her more hesitant towards new nannies/au pairs that enter the family:

Emily:	'In the beginning [when we first had au pairs], I was more like, I was more together with them all the time because then it was much more fun than it is now. For every au pair, I have held back more. One step at a time, I have become quieter and not like "Oh, what shall we do now?", more one step at a time. It's a bit sad.'
Researcher:	'And now you're getting another one I heard, they [the parents] are looking for someone for the fall.'
Emily:	'Mm.'
Researcher:	'How does that feel?'
Emily:	'Not that good really.'

The narratives of children who have experienced several break-ups and the re-entering of new nannies often entail stories like Emily's: of learning how to handle the 'nanny circle'. Some – like Emily – express rather strong negative emotions. Camilla, for example, talks about being very reluctant and even uncooperative when new nannies and au pairs arrive. "I want to know more about them first, before I tell them about me", she says:

Camilla:	'So, I can be a bit, like, talk back, be a bit cocky maybe, see how they react, before I react […] when I was little, then I was more like my siblings, but when we got Patricia [former nanny], my siblings started to play right away, and I sat in a corner being grumpy. And everything just … all the time, and she was like, "But come on now", and then, in the end, it became like, I could join them.'
Researcher:	'Has it been like this every time?'
Camilla:	'Carla was better.'

Camilla's reserved attitude is related to her experience of several turns in the 'nanny circle': she has had many nannies and au pairs involved in her life, and some of the break-ups have been hurtful, but especially the one from Carla, her favourite. In the interview, Camilla plays out an imagined conversation with a nanny who is leaving:

Camilla:	'You kind of, "But why did you come here in the first place?". Kind of. [...] "Yes, but you came here – you can't quit, can you?".'
Researcher:	'No, no.'
Camilla:	'And then we get a new one, just like, "But why, why can't she be with me?". And then you have to get to know another one, and another one, and another one, and after a while, in the end, it gets really difficult.'

While telling the interviewer this, Camilla says that she would not say this to anyone involved, not the nannies, au pairs or her parents, as she does not want to upset anyone. Camilla's narrative is full of emotions, especially when she talks about the break-ups and the 'getting to know' situations, and she has developed strategies to deal with this: she protects herself by being uncooperative and, from what she describes, probably really hard to handle for the one entering into a care situation with Camilla. Other children relate narratives in which emotions are less immediate. They describe having nannies and au pairs as an enterprise of learning to handle her more as a function or role. Ivan talks about it being hard in the beginning to accept a new au pair so soon after the old one has left, but, eventually, he has come to use his previous knowledge of having good au pairs as a blueprint for getting to know the new ones, he says:

Ivan:	'At first, I was sad because the other one had left, because we had had so much fun and everything, but then I got to know the new one, and then we started to have fun too, and that felt good, yeah.'
Researcher:	'Was it easy to get to know them or...?'
Ivan:	'As I remember it, yes it was, but I think, in the beginning, it was hard because when you're little, you are shyer when you meet new people. But when I got older and, like, when I had the last au pair, then it was, like, then I could get to know them in a rather good way, since I had, I had had good au pairs before.'

While arguing that he has better learned how to deal with au pairs, Ivan still says that the endings are hard: he compares them with his painful experience of having friends move away. Part of the learning process in the 'nanny circle' is to learn how not to get too emotionally involved so that the break-ups hopefully become easier. Still, the narratives testify to endings often being emotionally upsetting to the child. Some children are better at shielding themselves. One way of doing so is to actively obstruct the relationship with the new nanny or au pair, a strategy that, however, is hard to keep up in the long run since the child eventually has to allow her to get involved in his or her life, at least to some extent (unless the child's behaviour results in the nanny or au pair giving up her position, but this has, as far as we know, not happened in the families we met). Another strategy is to start treating the nanny or the au pair more like a 'role': letting previous experiences of 'good' relationships be the blueprint for how one engages in new ones, and playing one's own part as well as possible. The nanny circle, then, becomes less problematic as the child makes smaller emotional investments in each subsequent nanny or au pair.

Staying in contact

One way of making the exit of the nanny or au pair less painful is to stay in contact after she has quit her job in the family. Talking about the hardship of saying goodbye, Theo, for example, immediately stresses that "then it doesn't become as sad, when you stay in contact with them", and several children talk about former au pairs and nannies coming to visit – like Annelie, who is looking forward to her former au pair's upcoming visit – or of staying in contact through social media.

However, the children do not stay in contact with all nannies and au pairs. Sometimes, the nannies and au pairs and/or the parents are not interested in staying in touch, such as Emily's narrative of the sudden leaving of her au pair, and sometimes the children themselves do not want to keep the bonds with a nanny or an au pair, like Nomie earlier. Often, even relationships that are maintained fade away after a couple of years:

Researcher:	'Do you usually stay in contact with them afterwards?'
Karl:	'No, like … we have tried to stay in touch with some, or one in particular, because she was here for three years. She was really good and really nice.'
Researcher:	'And you liked her.'

Karl: 'Yes. My parents liked her too, and she was, she was very good, but it becomes a bit difficult when you've kind of not met in a very long time and you are, like, in different places.'

Children who want to stay in contact are often dependent on the parents' interest in helping out, at least if they are younger. Karl's narrative shows this: both he and his parents liked the particular nanny, and thus staying in contact with her was easier.

Staying in contact is thus neither easy nor always wanted. For many, there seems to be a 'learning curve' of handling the nanny circle of entering, leaving and entering again: staying in contact becomes less important when you have experienced a certain number of exits and new entrances. The specific memory of the person who has taken care of you seems to fade as a new person, doing similar chores, takes her place, sometimes literally, living in the same part of the house, doing the same things. The children's narratives of the 'nanny circle' do sometimes concur with parents' talk about children learning 'the system', as expressed in some parent interviews: several break-ups and introductions of new nannies and au pairs to fill the role lead some children to refrain from getting too emotionally involved with new nannies and au pairs. When this happens, the care situation itself changes: the expectation of personal closeness is supplanted by a view of the nanny and au pair as more a 'function' in the child's life. Some nannies and au pairs also adhere to this way of looking at their jobs: not getting emotionally involved to avoid getting hurt in break-ups is a well-known strategy of care workers in different contexts (Murray, 1998; Anderson, 2000), as well as for some nannies and au pairs in our study.

However – as do the nannies' and au pairs' narratives – the children's narratives attest to the hardship of this enterprise. Regardless of one's intention to avoid forming close bonds, when finding oneself in a care situation together, being involved in doings of care, it is very hard not to 'engage', at least, if the situation is to be considered good. Even children who say that they have learned not to engage tell about difficult break-ups. Furthermore, as the narrative of Camilla shows, resisting relationships when you find yourself in a care situation requires quite hard work on the part of the child, of withdrawing and being 'cocky' and grumpy. Although Camilla is convinced that she will never allow another nanny or au pair the same position of closeness as her favourite nanny, Carla, she still cannot keep a distance from the new ones in the long run. They are there, they care for her and, eventually, she has to enter into and take an active part in the care situation where they find themselves together.

Conclusion: children engaging with nannies and au pairs

Are the children being taken care of by nannies and au pairs the winners in the global care chains, or, at least, the winners of the restructured (and more neoliberal) Swedish welfare state? Are they experiencing their care situations as getting the "care gold", or as "more love for my child", as the parent Filippa expresses it in Chapter 3?

The children in this study are, in some sense, 'winners': their families' privileged position puts them in an advantageous place from the outset. Furthermore, they do get lots of attention from carers: the immense presence of nannies and au pairs in their everyday lives means that they probably get their needs met by adults to a larger extent than many other children in Sweden. That, however, does not mean that they are always happy with this way of arranging their care. The children's complex ways of acknowledging and concurring with, but also criticising, the parents' dedication to their work, and the ambiguous attitudes towards the presence of nannies and au pairs as a consequence of this, came through strongly in this study.

Most importantly, the narratives of children point towards the importance of the everyday mundane doings of care by nannies and au pairs: the care situation in which they find themselves, and in which they engage – together. In this, the 'doings' and the 'being there' of a nanny or au pair are intertwined: it is not enough, according to the children, for a nanny or au pair to just do the chores delegated to her by the parents. To be good, she has to do more. She has to show that she regards the child as special, that she *knows* the child and is willing to act upon that knowledge. Like the parents, the children have trouble defining the nannies' or au pairs' presence in their lives. The vocabulary that corresponds most to the children's understanding of her position is family terminology. The children expect closeness, as well as reciprocity: when they are acknowledged by the nanny or the au pair, when she engages with them, they are prepared to engage with her (Mason, 1996).

However, just as is the case of nannies and au pairs, that also means risking getting hurt. The narratives of the 'nanny circle' are strikingly more emotionally rich in the children's narratives, as compared to those of the parents, and more in line with the narratives of nannies and au pairs. Although the parents are, in some sense, right in assuming that the children 'learn' to handle break-ups, that it becomes less upsetting over the years and that the children do, indeed, see their parents as the 'constant' in their lives, memories of nannies and au pairs, of having to end and enter into new relationships, affect the children in our study. Most importantly, the memories of these experiences affect how the children engage in new care situations they are presented with. While they try to treat new nannies and au pairs more as a role – or as a means, 'not an end in themselves' (Tronto, 2002: 40) – in order to shield themselves from potential harm, in practice, this is very hard. The care situation necessitates engagement, from both partners involved in it.

6

Caring Complexities:
Care Situations and
Ambiguous Expectations

Care is at the centre of what we have described in the past three chapters: it is what parents expect nannies and au pairs to do when they hire them, and it is what nannies and au pairs see as the core part of their responsibility in the family. It is also what children expect of nannies and au pairs – that they should take care of them. However, at the same time, care is far from simple to put down in words; as DeVault (1991: 4) says, it is an activity that we 'know from experience but cannot easily label', an 'activity without a name, activity traditionally assigned to women, often carried out in family groups', although, in this case, the women are not 'really' part of the family group, nor are they completely outside.

Despite the intangible character of care, this chapter sets out to zoom in on it specifically. Drawing on and bringing together the narratives from the previous chapters, in the following, we will identify some key features in the *care situation* that children, nannies and au pairs find themselves in when doing care. We will also discuss how this situation corresponds with and diverges from the *expectations* of this care situation, formulated in ideals of the practice as an 'easy job'. This, then, finally, brings us to a discussion of *invisibility*: of what is obscured in the gap that emerges between the experience of an actual practice and the expectations of this practice. While all care doings can be argued to entail invisible doings, the care doings of nannies and au pairs are invisible in specific ways, and on many levels, simultaneously. Understanding this is crucial for understanding the particular precarity of this practice.

"It's the children who spend time with the nanny; the parents just employ her so they can be at work": the care situation according to children

In the preceding quote, 12-year-old Karl is pointing out the obvious: nannies and au pairs are hired to care for children, so they naturally spend time together. When Karl chooses to put emphasis on this in his interview, he is arguing for his right as a child to give his opinion and to talk about his experience of having nannies and au pairs: children, not parents, spend time with nannies and au pairs; thus, children are experts on this subject, in Karl's mind. In pointing this out, he also draws attention to the specific *care situation* in which nannies, au pairs and children meet. Parents may be the ones initiating, enabling and, to some extent, trying to orchestrate this situation, but the everyday care situation is done and experienced in a very direct sense by the nanny, au pair and the child, often alone, or in the company of siblings.

Looking at this care situation from the perspective of children, certain features emerge. First and foremost, it becomes obvious that *the doing of care chores and the 'being there' dimensions are intertwined* in children's understanding of nanny/au pair care. Furthermore, the 'doing' and the 'being there' are the primary *foundation upon which children 'reckon' their relationships* to the nannies and au pairs, that is, the ways in which children calculate, negotiate and make sense of this relationship (Mason and Tipper, 2008: 443; Davies, 2015). The relation to the nanny/au pair is, in one sense, imposed upon the child, but the *relationship* between them is formed in the midst of everyday doings. What the children expect of nannies and au pairs in the care situation is the emotional activities of care that Jennifer Mason (1996) has labelled *sentient activity*: that she attends to, notices and sees the child's needs, well-being, likes and dislikes, and that she makes use of this knowledge and acts upon it.

We see this in numerous examples in the data: how everyday tasks become so much more than the doing of a simple chore in the children's narratives. The everyday 'making of an afternoon snack', for example, stands out as a significant moment that nannies, au pairs and children share, when much more is going on than merely a simple serving of food, including tuning in to each other's moods and telling each other about what has happened during the day; as the child Ludwig said, knowing that this moment would take place made him "feel safe". This is a time when most parents need help since they are still at work, and as we saw in Chapter 3, it is a critical time – the "witching hour" – that many parents wish to escape. That this particular everyday moment reoccurs in the interviews with children, in talk and in drawings, is noteworthy.

The 'reckoning' of the relationship with the nanny/au pair takes place in these situations: *how* she is present when she carries out her chores becomes the foundation upon which the children negotiate their relationship with her. An au pair who is merely doing what she is supposed to according to the agreement with the parents is not doing enough. The ones who only serve the afternoon snack and then retreat to their rooms are not 'good' in the eyes of the children: to be good, they have to 'be there' in the moment. In all children's narratives, there is an expectation that the care situation should entail engagement on the part of the nanny, which should eventually also lead to a close relationship. The good nanny/au pair shows repeatedly, through her doings, that *the child is special to her*. Children see and feel, and express their expectation of, 'specialness' in different ways: in the nannies' and au pairs' willingness to play with them and talk to them about things that matter to them; in her proving to the child that she knows what the child likes, through initiating pleasurable activities such as baking or preparing the child's favourite food; and, sometimes, through her occasionally crossing the boundaries set by the parents, for example, through inviting the child into her private sphere. When nannies and au pairs do this, they show that they *are there for the child*. They notice the child and they interpret the child's needs and moods, likes and dislikes, and to do this, they need to have knowledge about *the particular child*, and have the ability and possibility of acting out of this knowledge. When they do not do it, when the care situation becomes just a performing of chores, it is not good enough, according to the children.

The children's narratives also attest to the active role that children have in the care situation: they do not passively accept the relations that are presented to them, but negotiate and evaluate who gets to be 'close' (Brannen et al, 2000; Brannen and Heptinstall, 2003; Ridge, 2007; Mason and Tipper, 2008; Marschall, 2014; Eldén, 2016). In addition, the children do not expect or see the 'specialness' in the relationship as operating only in one direction, as something nannies and au pairs should do to *them*. Arguably, the children are in a subordinate position in the sense that if the nanny or the au pair actively tries to avoid forming a close relationship, the children have limited possibilities of pursuing this themselves. However, when there is an engagement on the part of the nanny/au pair, the care situation also entails children's active engagement: children express interest in the particular nanny or au pair, and her wants and likes, just as they see her as interested in them. The care situation consists of reciprocal activities, where the 'recipient' of care is crucial, not only in the sense of being in a certain structural position ('dependent', 'superior' or symmetrical, as Wærness [1984: 189] argues), but also in the sense that the transaction requires and contains active doings of care by both parties (Fink, 2004; Eldén, 2016).

The reciprocity of the care situation, and the ways in which this situation requires the formation of a specific, relational and reciprocal commitment from both parties, comes out clearly in the narratives of children who have, indeed, actively tried to *not* form close relationships with nannies and au pairs. To protest against the introduction of a new nanny or au pair is an undertaking that requires lots of hard work, as attested to by the case of ten-year-old Camilla: keeping a distance from the new nanny, both physically and psychologically; refusing her access to carrying out the chores that she was supposed to; and being obstructive and even mean to the nanny or au pair. To be in a care situation *without* forming a specific and reciprocal bond requires active, and emotionally difficult, work of protest.

Arguably, children who have had many nannies and au pairs talk about situations and relationships that have *not* turned out to be particularly 'special', or, at least, were less emotionally imbued. We have suggested the term 'nanny circle' to capture the experience of entrances and exits of several nannies and au pairs in the lives of the children, and the attitude of precaution that some children expressed as a consequence of this: they learn not to get too involved. This, of course, changes the care situation. However, even in these cases, looking for some degree of specificity seems inevitable.

"It's not bad ... not hard ... a little bit hard": the care situation according to nannies and au pairs

While the children's narratives quite unanimously relate expectations of good nanny care as a reciprocal and emotional engagement in the doings and beings of the care situation, the narratives of nannies and au pairs are more ambiguous. On the one hand, nannies and au pairs are entering a 'job' that they expect to entail a number of chores that are thought to be easy and simple, as expressed both by themselves and also by parents. However, on the other hand, our interviews show that the care situation that nannies and au pairs find themselves in turns out to require much more complex and emotional doings than both the nannies, au pairs and parents usually expect.

This ambiguity presents itself clearly in the interviews. The narratives of nannies and au pairs entail a constant wavering between characterising their job as easy and with lots of "free time", and then describing everyday practices that by far extend the initial ideal regarding time, engagement and level of difficulty. In Ellie's narration, for example, the "sort of free time" that she says is supposed to take place during the day turns out to be a time when she is actually carrying out a lot of household chores. However, by describing this as "free time", Ellie is reproducing an ideal that is counter to what she is actually experiencing, something that also makes it difficult for her to understand why she is so tired at the end of her work day. The frequent reports about the 'unexpected' play a similar role in the nannies' and au pairs' narratives: when the narrating moves from describing how things 'ought to be' to talking about actual experiences – most obviously, accessed through the diaries – the 'unexpected' is always present. A child falls asleep in the car, with emotional turmoil as a result, which disrupts the whole evening; a mother does not come home at the agreed-upon time, which adds new chores for the nanny (and the child) to engage in, such as tucking in at night; and a child does not want to go to the daycare centre in the morning, which counters completely the idea of this being a 'simple task' – all of these situations have to be dealt with by the nanny or the au pair *in the moment*, and all of them require emotionally complex doings.

Indeed, it is in these reports about the everyday that the whole idea of the possibility of dividing up care into labour and emotional engagements proves to be impossible. In descriptions of the care situations in which the nannies and au pairs find themselves, as in the narratives of the children, the doing of care chores are inseparable from emotional doings. They are, again, of the kind that Jennifer Mason (1996) labels *sentient activity*. The "not hard" task of taking a child to daycare turns out to be not only "a little bit hard", as Caroline expresses it, but, indeed, full of emotional doings. To be able to read, and solve, the situation, the nanny or au pair has to have knowledge about the particular child: she has to interpret the child's behaviour and think through and come up with a solution that takes into consideration not only her own relationship to the child, but also the child's – and her – relationship to the parents.

In addition to diverging from the image of the practice as 'easy', within the care situation, there is also often a worry of whether the nanny's or au pair's thought-to-be appropriate solutions will meet the approval of the parents. Descriptions of being in a situation and feeling that it requires a certain form of action, but then feeling unsure of whether one is really allowed to act accordingly, reoccur in the nannies' and au pairs' narratives. Sometimes, they are told explicitly by the parents that their actions are not appropriate, as in the case of Gloria, whose host parents objected to her letting the children use tablets. In other cases, nannies and au pairs know what the parents expect and conform to this when parents are present but then continue with their own solutions behind the parents' backs.

The narratives of the nannies and au pairs attest to not only emotional doings ingrained in practical doings, but also a wide *variety of emotional doings*, both positively and negatively marked. The care situation seems to *require* these: to do care in a way that 'works', the nanny and the au pair need to 'be in the moment', 'know' and take in the particular situation, and act and react accordingly (DeVault, 1991; Mason, 1996). This, in turn, becomes the foundation for *the specific* relationship between herself and the child, which is also required for the care situation to be experienced as good. Here, emotional closeness, often positive in nature, is also common.

The necessity of emotional closeness in care situations becomes most obvious in narratives where nannies and au pairs are explicitly trying to *not* engage. Nannies and au pairs who have been in several care situations and thereby developed close relationships that they have been forced to break up talk about how, when entering new care situations, they try to keep a distance. However, to keep a distance is hard. Nannies and au pairs talk about constantly having 'their' children in mind, even when they consciously wish to have a more professional attitude towards the employing families. Similarly to the children, for a nanny or an au pair to keep a distance when she finds herself in a care situation requires hard work: having to force herself not to think about, sense and act according to what she senses is necessary in the moment. If she succeeds in this, she is often left with the feeling of not really doing her job, despite the fact that she is doing all of the chores expected of her.

The available language to describe the job of nannying and au pairing is the term 'easy'. This narrative constantly interferes with, disrupts and downplays accounts about everyday caring situations, testifying to complexity and difficult emotional doings (DeVault, 1991). Consequently, the nannies and au pairs end up relating that 'this is not for me'. 'I'm not really a nanny' was a recurrent utterance in the interviews, 'it doesn't fit me'. Failure to live up to the idea of 'easy' is always seen as an individual flaw, as when Ellie blames herself for not being able to manage everything in the designated time without being exhausted; it is her own fault, she says, as she is probably too slow. This is also seen when Gloria, who did, indeed, express criticism of her host parents – they "don't see all the things I do with the children", she said – still has problems pinning down for herself what she actually *does* when she spends time with the children. However, somehow, Gloria still knows, in her mind and in her body, that the care situations she has experienced have been intense and demanding.

"She always reminded me, she was, like, engaged in all this too": parents' ambiguous expectations of nanny and au pair care

The parents' descriptions of the practice of nanny and au pair care are, as one could expect, not as close to the actual doings as those of the other actors as they are often not present in the actual care situations taking place (although they are, as we have seen, often present in the minds of nannies and au pairs). However, they do have expectations of the nanny and au pair care that they imagine will take place.

The parents, on the one hand, rely heavily on the assumption that care can be divided into 'labour' and 'emotion'. When buying the service of a nanny or an au pair, there is an underlying assumption of the possibility of separating care into 'manageable blocks of time' (Tronto, 2002: 44), and 'spiritual' and 'menial' work (Roberts, 1997). These understandings are present in parents' talk about inviting someone else to do parts of the care as not in any way threatening to their own position as 'the most important' for their children (see also Macdonald, 2010). Some parents even distinguished the same caring chore as having different meaning when it was carried out by the au pair and by the parents: the au pair's doing of this chore was constructed as a basic necessity, while the parents' doing of the same chore was seen as quality time, as a "relaxed and enjoyable" moment for parents and children to share. Understandings of care as labour/emotion were also present in descriptions of nanny and au pair work as following a list of clearly defined chores, sometimes provided by the parents in written lists and schedules, sometimes in verbal instructions. As in the case of the nannies and au pairs, the work was described in terms of an 'easy job' with lots of freedom and opportunities to decide when and where to carry out one's chores.

On the other hand, the parents did not really adhere to this narrative themselves; they expected more, and they did expect emotional activities of the sort Mason (1996) labels sentient activity. As in the interviews with nannies and au pairs, these expectations came out more indirectly, in talk about practices, as well as in talk about 'good and bad' nannies. The extensive quotes from the mother Nelly in Chapter 3, for example, showed the constant wavering between characterising the au pair's job as easy and then, when describing the 'normal everyday situation', revealing that the au pair's responsibilities in everyday practices were comprehensive, including complex activities such as thinking "about everything" and keeping in mind and remembering what Nelly herself often forgot about the children's activities and needs. The au pair is "a real household manager", as Nelly expressed it. It is, indeed, this quality that makes the au pair 'good': she knows the children's everyday world and takes it upon herself to do everything that the situation requires. The ability of 'project leading' distinguishes a good au pair from a not so good one in the parents' narratives, as the example of Ofelia showed: while her first au pair did, indeed, do all the things Ofelia asked her to do, "she never did anything extra", she did not realise she should start the laundry, but just performed the requested chores and then retreated into her room. In contrast, later au pairs 'engaged' in the everyday caring situation and saw what needed to be done, sometimes even before Ofelia saw it herself, and thus relieved Ofelia from always being the "one at the steering wheel". Expectations like these were rarely stated explicitly to the nannies and au pairs; instead, they were a kind of unspoken background assumption that the nannies and au pairs were expected to just 'get'. While some seem to do that – the good ones in the eyes of the parents – others do not.

Care situations and sentient activities

In the previous descriptions, we can discern a movement within the narratives from the different categories of actors presented to us in this study. In the children's narration about nanny and au pair care, the care situation is quite clear: children expect and experience doings of care in their everyday life that entail sentient activity. Moving to the narratives of nannies and au pairs, the sentient activity character of the care situation is present here too, but with the added component of parents' views of how the care situation should be, and the more general ideal of the nanny/ au pair practice as 'easy'. The parents' narratives, finally, also and often strongly reproduce the ideal of 'easy', as well as relying on the possibility of dividing up care into 'emotion' and 'labour' while, at the same time, making implicit demands of sentient activity entailing emotional activities far exceeding the ideal of easy.

In the narratives of children, nannies and au pairs, it becomes clear that when entering into a care situation, nannies, au pairs and children are engaging in what Wærness (1984) calls the 'rationality of care': a form of 'knowing' based upon *practice*, in contrast to universalised knowledge. Importantly, this is not to be conflated with intuition (which would lead us back to essentialist notions of women's innate caring capabilities). On the contrary, knowledge about how to care in a good way is acquired through *being in* caring situations. However, learning to care is never a once and for all acquired knowledge since the character of the care situation is always shifting and changing: the ability to be flexible and adapt to changing situations is an inherent characteristic of the rationality of care (Wærness, 1984: 197).

In the narratives of children, nannies and au pairs, it becomes obvious that universalised knowledge of 'how to make an afternoon snack' or 'how to take a child to daycare' is never enough: for a good care situation to take place, *specific* knowledge is needed, and more than that, one has to be constantly prepared to 'relearn' as circumstances change. At the same time, the experience of pain from break-ups – the 'nanny circle' – makes nannies, au pairs and children hesitant to engage in this process. Instead, the lesson learned from previous care situations becomes one of restricting oneself: for the nannies and au pairs to try to separate out the practical care doings from the emotional, and for the children to refrain from emotional engagements and start to treat the (new) nanny or au pair more like a 'function' in their lives. However, our narratives still show that is it extremely difficult *not* to engage emotionally when *being in the moment* of the care situations; therefore, despite their efforts, they find themselves engaging emotionally again in the end.

What is it, then, within these care situations that requires this specific engagement? In her studies of childcare workers, Susan B. Murray (1998) argues that the many hours of routinely and emotionally intensive interaction that caregivers and children engage in every day result in caregivers developing specific 'situational identities'. Caring for children, and especially small children, means engaging in relationships where the other party – the child – is making 'heavy emotional demands' and engaging in the relationship as if it were '"naturally" occurring (read: not work related)', Murray (1998: 156) argues. Similarly, in her studies of children's reckoning of family and kinship relations, Hayley Davies (2011) emphasises the importance of physical proximity for children's personal relationships: 'seeing' others and having face-to-face interaction is crucial for children as it allows for 'a multi-sensorial experience including sharing time, talking, (often unconscious) observations of one another's actions and interactions, facial expressions, appearances, tone of voice', which provide 'a context for children to develop a holistic knowledge of a family member's character and appearance' (Davies, 2011: 20; see also Mason and Tipper, 2008). In the case of children, nannies and au pairs, the everyday routine interactions and the multi-sensorial experience of proximity is there, *in* the care situation, and the situation itself seems to necessitate closeness, despite the fact that the person doing care is not 'family'. The reoccurring use and negotiations of family terminology, especially from children, is a sign of this since, as Murray (1998: 163) argues, there are no other cultural scripts available to capture these kinds of relationships.

However, to argue for the importance of everyday interactions and physical closeness is not the same as arguing that the doing of care *labour* results in the development of *emotions* and feelings of closeness, or even love, which, as we saw in Chapter 2, was the recurrent argument in global care chain research. Indeed, feelings of love do occur between nannies, au pairs and children, and these can and are sometimes exploited by parents in demanding overtime and engagements beyond agreed-upon working contracts. However, this assumption, by reproducing the idea of the possibility of separating labour from emotion, misses out on the diversity of emotional activities in care situations that nannies, au pairs and children engage in.

As we have argued throughout this book, in narratives of care situations, 'doings', 'beings' and 'reckonings' are entangled. The care situations that the children and the nannies/au pairs find themselves in are full of emotional activities. It is not the case that a nanny or an au pair starts out by doing 'emotionless' labour chores and then develops feelings for the children in her care, or that the child passively receives the care services of nannies and au pairs and then eventually starts to have feelings for her. Instead, emotions are there from the start, not just in the sense of the actors harbouring different feelings towards the people they engage with (which they, of course, also do), but, more importantly, because the nannies, au pairs and children engage in emotional activities. In her everyday doings, the nanny/au pair is deeply involved in 'noticing/interpreting/being attuned to the moods/needs/ likes and dislikes/relationships' of the children in her care (Mason, 1996: 27). This engagement occurs, for example, in her greeting of a child coming home from school in the afternoon. It crystallises itself in the very practical moment of 'making an afternoon snack', a simple feeding practice that is, indeed, loaded with so much more than the physical doing of preparing the snack: knowing what the child likes, interpreting his/her mood and trying to tune in to this to create a nice (or, in some cases, just bearable) moment (DeVault, 1991). For a nanny or an au pair, this activity is profoundly intertwined with 'thinking through/working out/organising' relationships between herself and the child, as well as herself and the parents – and, in addition, thinking through and taking into consideration how what she does or does not do affects the child's relationship with the parents (Mason, 1996: 27). Again, returning to the afternoon snack example, to serve appropriate food, to make sure that the children do their homework, get off to their activities or engage in 'qualitative activities', and often also to engage in other household chores – all to the liking of the parents – while simultaneously *trying to solve the care situation of the moment* is hard work.

These 'thinking activities', and the ability to act upon them, constitute the core of the care situation. They are inherently emotional, and not in the sense that they involve only positive feelings of love; on the contrary, they are often difficult and gruelling. In fact, without these emotional doings, care is not really happening. This is the kind of care doing that nannies, au pairs and children find themselves doing. It is also, as we saw, an implicit expectation on the part of the parents: the good nanny/au pair 'sees what needs to be done' without being told.

However, these doings are missing in the ideal description of nanny and au pair work as 'easy'. In fact, the narrating of 'easy' plays an important part in obscuring the practice, both for parents and for nannies and au pairs themselves. Marjorie DeVault (1991: 228) argues that there is a discursive gap when it comes to narrating about 'everyday household work': there is no adequate language available to capture the complexity of the activities that women engage in when doing care. It is doings that we all – and especially women – are very familiar with as they are so taken for granted and necessary for survival. However, the lack of a language to capture all the complex and emotional doings that are involved results in the practices being obscured (DeVault, 1991: 227). The discursive labelling of nanny and au pair care as 'easy', reproduced in the framework surrounding the practice, as well as by parents, nannies and au pairs, makes a large part of the doings in the care situations that nannies and au pairs are involved in invisible. The sentient activity of care is thus simultaneously *inevitable* in the sense that it is a necessary component of the caring situation that children, nannies and au pairs engage in, and, at the same time, *invisible* as it is outside of the constantly reproduced ideal of the practice being easy, outside the explicit 'role' of nanny/au pair and also, since in *itself*, in the broader societal context, it is a doing that is rarely acknowledged. This clash between experience and expectations is, we argue, what makes the nanny/au pair position precarious.

Invisible doings of care

A key argument in the early feminist care debates concerned the invisibility of care work: as women were seen to do care work as a 'natural' extension of their caring psyche, the hard labour of caring was obscured (Finch and Groves, 1983). The labour–emotion dichotomy was introduced to counter and demystify this invisibility (Graham, 1983), as well as to reveal the ways in which asymmetry – especially between the genders – is built into and reproduced through assumptions of care (Wærness, 1984). However, in its endeavour to make visible the hard work of care that women do, feminist care scholarship, as a consequence of a too singular focus on labour, left emotions unproblematised (Mason, 1996). This, in turn, led to other forms of care doings still being neglected: the 'activity without a name', in DeVault's (1991: 4) thinking, or the activities labelled sentient activity by Mason (1996; see also Macdonald, 2010: 110). These care doings are, as Mason has argued, not only invisible to the ones doing them, but also often very demanding and exhausting. In fact, as we have shown earlier, the invisibility of, and the lack of an adequate language to describe, these doings *adds* to the experience of them being demanding and difficult. From the perspectives of the nannies and au pairs, the expectations of care as sentient activity are both 'sensed' by them through the parents' ways of reacting towards what they do in the family, and also directly experienced as necessary because the care situation in itself demands this kind of care to be done.

This represents the most fundamental way in which the doings of nanny and au pair care in families are invisible: care as sentient activity is so taken for granted, so hard to 'pin down', that it rarely shows. It is the kind of doing that often only becomes visible when it is missing (DeVault, 1991: 228), as in the parents' comparison of good and bad nannies/au pairs, or that which is traceable when people are invited to talk about practices, beyond ideal descriptions of how it 'should be'.

In the case of nannies and au pairs, their doings of care as sentient activity become even more invisible since the nannies and au pairs are entering into a role that, at the outset, relies heavily on the dichotomy of labour–emotion, and their main contribution is thought to be in the labour part of the dichotomy. They are hired to solve the 'jigsaw puzzle of life' of the family, to do all the chores of picking up at daycare, providing meals, cleaning, doing laundry and so forth – all of which is portrayed by the parents as being 'easy', and also often so described by the nannies and au pairs themselves. The expectations of all those other things – all the emotional doings – only emerge implicitly in the narratives of the parents, and always with underlying assumptions that the emotional doings, and the relationships that are constituted through these, are not *as* important, or *as* emotional, as parental (or other kinship) relationships. The discrepancy between the experience of the care situation, on the one hand, and, on the other, the surrounding frame of doing easy chores and solving a jigsaw puzzle makes the emotional doings of care even more difficult to identify and talk about.

Another contributing reason for the invisibility of the care activities is the gendered association of women and 'natural' abilities of caring: '[D]omestic, family, household, and bodily work' of 'housework, cooking, mothering, and childcare' is predominantly associated with women

(Mason, 1996: 30). Since it is an activity that is 'skilled' in the sense that one needs training in situations where care happens (Wærness, 1984: 197), and since *being in* these situations is most often experienced by women, care, and especially expectations of the sentient activity dimensions in care, is gendered.

In our interviews, the gendered character of expectations of sentient activity is not talked about explicitly. However, assumptions about care as a female activity come through indirectly, for example, when the parents talk about the family situation before the hiring of nannies and au pairs, of the couples ending up in a 'traditionally' gendered sharing of household responsibilities and also of different expectations being placed upon them as fathers and mothers. The nanny and the au pair are, in this sense, stepping in to do work that is assumed to be 'female' from the outset. This is also visible in the metaphors used to describe her work. When the mothers in our study (sometimes jokingly, sometimes more seriously) refer to the nanny or the au pair as an 'extra wife' who can take on – or at least share with them – the role of 'household manager', the gendered associations are implied: it is a woman who is most fitting to fill this position.[1] When reflecting upon the fact that they have only employed female nannies and au pairs (all of the 83 nannies and au pairs hired by families in this study have been women), most parents see this as accidental. While they are theoretically positive towards the idea of hiring male nannies and au pairs, they say that they have not really thought about it, or that it has never come up as an option since they have not seen the advertisements of male nannies or au pairs. This reflects our observations as well: there are very few men posting adverts on au pair sites, and few men on the nanny companies' websites.[2] In that sense, the position of nanny and au pair is gendered, and simultaneously obscured as being gendered: only women are available; thus, hiring a woman is the obvious – but not conscious – choice. The 'extra wife' is a young woman, and this just seems appropriate and natural. The implicit expectations of sentient activity that we have identified attest to expectations of emotional doings that very much approximate the traditional expectations of wives and mothers (DeVault, 1991: 4).

However, compared to the role of 'mother' and 'wife', the nanny/ au pair cannot make any claims on the status of 'family', and this is yet another dimension that adds to the invisibility of the care doings of nannies and au pairs. Regardless of the fact that her 'doings' and 'beings' in the care situation put her in a position where the children often understand her in 'family-like' terms, the underlying deal is that she is not: she is employed for a short period of time, and although some parents talk about staying in touch, most report relationships fading out (or, in some cases, being abruptly ended). Nannies and au pairs are aware of this too, and for several, especially for the ones who have been doing this job for some time, trying to stay out of becoming 'part of the family' is key. Given some parents' use of 'part of the family' as a means of demanding overtime and engagement beyond agreed-upon chores, this is not at all surprising. However, as we have shown, even in the cases when nannies and au pairs explicitly try to shield themselves from being 'part of family', they are still dependent on the parents' labelling of their position, and still have to handle the 'family-like' expectations in the care situation, expressed especially by the children. Mason (1996) argues that care as sentient activity is specific to the sphere of family and kin relationships. The doing of this care by nannies and au pairs is, then, a doing that is expected in family and kin relationships, while simultaneously being an activity carried out by someone who *is not* family. Her position of being in-between – neither employed, nor part of the family – makes her sentient doings of care even less visible.[3]

The invisibility of the care doings of nannies and au pairs are further linked to the specific, precarious structural positions that these women find themselves in, related to age, migration/ethnicity and social class. Housework defines women, as Bridget Anderson (2000) has argued, those who do dirty work and those who do not, and this arrangement is marked by, and reproduces, class and ethnicity (Roberts, 1997; Tronto, 2002). While ethnicity and class are very rarely discussed explicitly by the parents or the children in our study, there are assumptions being reproduced in and through the practice of who is 'best suited' for this kind of work, not least visible on the state level in the prerogatives for initiating and encouraging the domestic service market in the first place (Kvist and Peterson, 2010) (this will be discussed further in Chapter 7). Nannies and au pairs are young women who, through their background, but, most importantly, through their relative positioning within the practice of nannying/au pairing, are in a structural position subordinate to the parents (Skeggs, 2004). This puts them in situations where the experienced problems become extra difficult for them to verbalise. The precarity of the situation of domestic workers has been the focus of many scholars within the field of global care chain research (see, for example, Parrenas, 2001; Stenum, 2010; Lutz, 2011; Bikova, 2017), and the lack of – or weak – frameworks regulating the work also in Sweden is striking (Calleman, 2010, 2011; Anving and Eldén, 2016). Some of the narratives in our study add to the array of accounts in the literature of fear related to one's subordinate position: narratives about feeling obliged to do not-agreed-upon (and sometimes dangerous) chores for fear of losing the job; narratives of not getting paid or not getting the agreed-upon benefits;

and, though rarely, but still occurring, narratives of sexual abuse (Gavanas, 2013). Arguably, some nannies and au pairs in our study, mostly the ones coming from poorer countries outside of the European Union (EU), are in a more precarious position than others as they are more dependent upon the situation in the family working out since losing the job would have severe consequences not only for themselves, but also for their family back home. Also, the formal character of the work carried out by nannies through nanny companies should safeguard better working conditions as compared to the privately organised arrangements of au pairs. However, nannies in our study also talk about job insecurity, and the boundaries between 'formal' and 'informal' are not always clear (Gavanas, 2010).

The subordinate structural position coming from the class and migration/ ethnicity position of nannies and au pairs, all of which have been in focus in previous research within the global care chain field, contributes to the invisibility of the practice. However, a thorough understanding of the precarious situation also needs to take into consideration how these work together with the earlier identified *invisibilities inherent in the everyday practice of doing care*. This precarity exists regardless of one's structural position when entering into the practice of being a nanny or an au pair. To fully understand this, one needs to acknowledge that gender is still a primary organisational principle of care doings, and especially so regarding the emotional care doings of sentient activity. Children expect and experience care situations full of sentient activity, and nannies and au pairs do all those things without being acknowledged for them; in fact, these doings are actively kept invisible through the labelling of nanny and au pair work as 'easy'. It is through these doings that the nanny and the au pair keep the family going: she solves the jigsaw puzzle of life and she becomes an invisible glue that makes the pieces stay firmly together. In doing this, she is 'doing family'.

7

Conclusion:
Doing Nanny Families

By doing the work of 'wife' and 'mother', women quite
literally produce family life from day to day, through their
joint activities with others. By 'doing family' in traditional
ways, household members sustain and reproduce the
'naturalness' of prevailing arrangements. (DeVault, 1991: 13)

'I feel like ... I'm really into this everyday life, thinking
and sometimes feeling like a mother.' (Ellie, au pair)

The everyday care that nannies and au pairs – and other domestic workers
– do in families has been left off the radar of most family sociology. This
is remarkable given the actual predominance of the practice in many
Western/Northern societies, and the growing prevalence in Nordic
countries. Global care chain research, which has, indeed, brought this
phenomenon into focus, has left assumptions about 'family' and 'care'
under-problematised in many instances. Furthermore, in both strands of
research, the perspective of the children receiving care has largely been
missing. In this last chapter, we want to, first, elaborate on the necessity
of including the analysis of nanny and au pair care in the theorising of
family, as well as argue for the need for a critical analysis of the family in
global care chain research. This is necessary to get at the ways in which
this practice is 'doing inequality', in and through family doings, which
is the second focus in this chapter. This, in turn, leads us back to the
question raised at the beginning of the book: what is happening to the
ideals of gender and social equality, in welfare states such as Sweden,
when new and privatised ways of 'doing family' are introduced? Finally,
we conclude with a discussion of the delicate question of 'good care': is
nanny and au pair care good for children?

The invisible glue of the 'good family'

When outlining the main arguments in his theorising on 'doing family', David Morgan (1996) put the everyday at centre stage: the 'whole set of what appears to be trivial or even meaningless activities', those activities that seem 'unremarkable, hardly worth talking about', are *constitutive* of family, he argued (Morgan, 2011: 5). Care is a significant part of this doing of family (Morgan, 1996). In fact, caring – and especially the emotional doings of care labelled sentient activity by Jennifer Mason (1996) – is a form of doing of family that is particularly often seen as 'hardly worth talking about', something that is attributed to the gendering of the practice, as something women do 'naturally' (DeVault, 1991). As we argued in Chapter 6, when 'other women' besides the wives and mothers identified by DeVault (1991) in the earlier quote are doing these caring acts, they become even more invisible. This prompts us to ask: what should be the grounds for analysing nanny and au pair positions? Are they, through their doing of care, also doing family, despite their not being 'part of the family'?

The critical re-evaluation of the sociological care scholarship of the 1980s rightfully identified the theoretical blindness towards inequalities other than gender, and the related preoccupation with the role of women in the family as wives and mothers. Graham (1991) and Tronto (2002, 2010), both using the examples of domestic work to debunk the flaws in theorising on care, argued for the need for broader concepts of care beyond 'the family' (Morgan, 1996: 103). However, recognising that non-kin actors, such as domestic workers, do care in families does not diminish the importance of analysing 'family', or gendered – and racialised and classed – doings of care *within* 'the family'.

Actually, arguing that the recognition of the doing of care by domestic workers means moving the analysis 'beyond family' ends up reproducing a quite static and narrowly kin-based definition of family. Our data counter this: the doings of nannies and au pairs are often being narrated and understood in and through family terminology, especially by the children, and if we are to take seriously the fluidity of the concept, this needs to be considered. In addition, positioning the work of domestic workers as something that is best understood as a doing of care 'beyond family' means failing to acknowledge that their situation is not only dependent upon structures *outside* of the care situation, such as class and migratory position, but also on *assumptions of care in families*. The work done by nannies and au pairs is not just a placing of a paid worker in the setting of a family, where the domestic worker's situation should be analysed as a doing of care beyond family, while the arena she works in, the family, should be seen as consisting of actors doing other (though similar) care doings best analysed by a focus on 'the family'. Instead, her doings are also 'doing family'.

To get at the ways in which nannies and au pairs do family, one could argue that, in this study, we have made use of one of the 'tricks' suggested by Becker (1998): if two different categories of people are involved in doing similar things, new insights can be made from starting out in the practice and for a moment disregarding the category (see also Morgan, 1996, 2011). Through looking at the practice of nannies and au pairs in families, we have been able to show how their doings of care both entail and resemble 'traditional' doings of care by wives and mothers, and how it departs from this. We have been able to show that much of the invisible care work previously done by female family members and kin, in 'producing' and reproducing the 'traditional family' (DeVault, 1991: 13), is still expected to be done but now through implicit expectations of 'good' nannies and au pairs.

This has been visible in all of the preceding chapters in parents' talk about nannies and au pairs stepping in and taking on all the practicalities of everyday life, of her presence being the solution to the 'jigsaw puzzle of life', to the reduction of stress and the making of a harmonious everyday life. It has been visible in the narratives of nannies and au pairs in their talk about the carrying out of chores placed upon them by parents, and in the children's narratives about all the different things that nannies and au pairs do, for them and for their families, in their everyday lives. The doing of care by nannies and au pairs creates the *care situation*: the everyday situation where the 'trivial', 'unremarkable' chores turn out to be intertwined with – in fact, inseparable from – emotional, sentient activities necessary for the doing of care.

Our inclusion of children's perspectives on nanny and au pair care in their everyday lives provided us with a piece that has been missing: it was through their narratives that the contours of the care situation could be fully captured. Previous studies of nannies and au pairs have, indeed, pointed towards experiences of conflicting demands, and the recurrent narrative of nannies and au pairs becoming 'too' close to children, starting to feel positive feelings of love and commitment. However, our practice-focused narratives of children, nannies and au pairs attest to the flaws of the dichotomy of labour and emotion: the doings of care expected from nannies and au pairs by children, the doings they engage in together in the care situation, are emotional activities from the outset. This, in turn, stands in contrast to the expectations and discursive framing of the practice, which rely heavily on the possibility of dividing up care into labour and emotion, or 'menial' and 'spiritual'. These discrepancies are felt by the nanny and the au pair in her everyday doings, expressed in feelings of being overwhelmed by work, of not really understanding why the 'easy' job she has taken upon herself is making her exhausted, in feelings of 'love' for the children coexisting with more ambiguous feelings of them being a bit 'difficult to handle', and in feelings of nannying or au pairing as 'not being for me, really'. It is also visible in children's disappointment with nannies and au pairs who are not 'really there' – who do not engage with them, who do not 'see' them – and their appreciation of the nannies and au pairs who do all that. The nanny and the au pair are, as we argued in Chapter 6, doing much of (sometimes all) the visible and invisible work of care previously done by wives and mothers, and, in this sense, they are doing family. However, since they never fully achieve the status of 'part of the family', their doings are invisible.

This is also why it does not work to characterise the nanny/au pair either as 'employed' or as 'part of the family'. This dichotomy is used both by the actors involved and by researchers in trying to understand the situation that domestic workers find themselves in. The most common argument in global care chain research is that by moving between the two, employers exercise their power – by claiming that a domestic worker is part of the family, more labour can be demanded (Anderson, 2000) – and this did occur in some instances in our study too (Anving and Eldén, 2016). However, more commonly, the dichotomy is used, especially by the children, as a way of 'reckoning' the relationship to a nanny or an au pair. 'Part of the family' becomes a framework for understanding her doing and 'being' in the family, and is often used, in addition, as a way of demarcating closeness and inclusion on the part of the children. The strongest feature coming through in our interviews with parents, nannies and au pairs is the discomfort with the labels: to call a nanny or an au pair 'employed' seems wrong, as does situating her as 'part of the family'.

This discomfort points towards the fact that she is involved in the *invisible doings of family*. Her doing of care – all the sentient activity she does and is (sometimes implicitly) expected to do – places her in a position where she is reproducing the family, in both visible and invisible ways, just as women in families have traditionally done (DeVault, 1991). When 'part of the family' is only understood as a 'feeling' that can be exploited, like love in the labour–love dichotomy, the complexity of 'family' is missed out, and the ways in which nannies and au pairs *do family* – regardless of how they are labelled – stays invisible. Irrespective of whether she is included as 'part of the family' by an employing family, and irrespective of whether she sees herself as 'part of the family', she is 'part of *doing* family'.

The parents in our study use different metaphors to describe the nanny's/au pair's function in their family: she takes on the "buffer time", as Vera says; she is our "elastic band", in the words of Ann-Katrin; and she is an "extra pair of arms", in the words of Jessica, ready to reach out and help whenever and wherever needed. Another metaphor has emerged in our minds during this research project, namely, that of *glue* (see also Macdonald, 2010: 171). Like glue, the doings of nannies and au pairs fill in and paste together the cracks and gaps that would otherwise materialise in everyday life between the demands of work and family. She makes sure that it all works out, that children get to their activities, that food gets bought, cooked and put on the table – she reminds both parents and children of what needs to be done to keep the everyday running smoothly. She "pushes us forward", as the child Ludwig said, she "is there" and makes the home feel "safe". Her doings glue the family together; they reduce the number of conflicts in the family, both between mothers and fathers, and also between parents and children. Some nannies and au pairs see their function as glue quite clearly, and they sometimes take pride in their ability to help the family realise the good life, and to create "family time", as Olivia expressed it. Often, this also involves having knowledge of when to make oneself invisible, when to withdraw oneself and leave the family alone (Macdonald, 2010: 118). However, more often, the doings are in a more general sense invisible, as, indeed, all sentient activity is. Like glue, her doings are only noticeable when they are missing, and the pieces start to fall apart again. The nanny/au pair doing of family is thus, to a large extent, an invisible glue that makes a certain kind of family practice – and family ideal – possible.

Gender equality and stress-free parenting: inequalities between families

The doings of care by nannies and au pairs make possible a very particular kind of family life. Throughout this book, and especially in the chapter focusing on parents, several ingredients within the family life that nannies and au pairs enable in Swedish families have been identified.

The dual-career family, with its *reformulated gender-equality ideal*, is one of them. The parents in our study are doing their families in a context wherein gender equality is a taken-for-granted 'good thing'. As we saw in the introductory chapter, since the 1960s, gender equality has been an explicit political aim of Swedish family politics, and this is reflected in families' everyday lives, in the positive affirmation of the ideal by both women and men. However, these ideals are difficult to realise, and women are still responsible for most of the care work at home (Ahlberg et al, 2008; Grönlund and Halleröd, 2008; Roman and Peterson, 2011). Lack of gender equality in practice was also one of the primary arguments for the proponents of a tax deduction for domestic services: to give women the same opportunities to succeed at work, they needed to be relieved of care work at home, it was argued.

This argument is very much embraced by the parents employing nannies and au pairs. Indeed, it seems to work well: both the mothers and the fathers in our study are engaged in very successful and demanding careers. The trap of falling into traditional gender roles is avoided since having a nanny or an au pair means that "you don't need to choose" who is going to step back from his or her career, as the father Leif says. Thereby, a significant factor of conflict within the couple is avoided: both careers and couple relationships are enhanced, maybe even saved. However, at the same time, the hiring of nannies and au pairs also makes fathers less gender equal in the sense that they need to do less care work at home. This points to the ways in which the politically encouraged growth in the market for paid domestic work, and the practice of hiring nannies and au pairs, has reformulated the ideal – and practice – of gender equality in families: from dual earner/dual carer to dual earner/privately outsourced care. It has made gender equality all about the earner part of the dichotomy, about a woman's right to have a career on the same terms as a man, and it has done so in a way that makes the care part even more invisible (Gunnarsson, 2013: 51). When care is delegated to someone else, this not only signals a devaluation of the practice as such (Roberts, 1997; Anderson, 2000), but also makes much of the doings of care – the sentient activity – more invisible, as we argued in Chapter 6. The invisible glue of nannying and au pairing is what enables the parents to pursue two careers, and realise the reformulated ideal of gender equality: the parents manage to solve the jigsaw puzzle of life without compromising their work ambitions – and are thus 'equal'.

To draw on the au pair Ellie's and Marjorie DeVault's quotes introducing this chapter, by taking over parts of 'the work of "wife" and "mother"', nannies and au pairs are 'producing family' in a 'traditional way', and 'sustaining and reproducing the "naturalness" of prevailing arrangements' (DeVault, 1991: 13). As Tronto argued (2002: 47), they become a means to reproduce the practice of a traditional patriarchal family, while obscuring the fact that this is, in fact, what is done. The gendered division of labour is maintained; it is still women – although other women – who do the care work at home, but the ideology portrayed outwardly is that of gender equality. In the case of Sweden, this is very clear: this 'traditional' – but now invisible – arrangement saves the strong positive discourse of the gender-equal couple, while hiding its economic privilege: only well-off families can afford to buy domestic services.

Another, very positively framed, doing of family that is enabled by the hiring of nannies and au pairs is the possibility of creating an *everyday life situation without stress and conflict*. This, the parents argue, makes them into *better parents*: more satisfied at work, less stressed out and ready to engage in and have quality time with the children during the times that they spend together.

The parents' delegation of care to nannies and au pairs relies heavily on the assumption of the possibility of dividing care into labour and emotion, and menial and spiritual (Roberts, 1997). The parents, as the primary and most important persons in the lives of their children, have an overarching responsibility and a position of being in control and orchestrating the caring framework where nannies, au pairs and children find themselves. The parenting parts 'kept' by the parents are thought to be primarily in the emotional or spiritual parts of care, and while they do, indeed, engage in and do everyday care chores – some more than others – being relieved from the mundaneness of the everyday is crucial in becoming a better parent.

The kind of parenting that is made possible through this is, in a sense, paradoxical: it is simultaneously characterised by enhanced possibilities of controlling the care situation, and, at the same time, by more distant and detached parenting. In her study of nannies, au pairs and their employer mothers in the US, Cameron Lynne Macdonald (2010) argues that the primary reason for the hardship experienced in these situations by both parties is motherhood ideologies of intense, competitive mothering: 'child-centered, expert-guided, emotionally absorbing, labor intensive, and financially expensive' mothering (Hays, 1996: 69). This is coupled with ideas of 'blanket accountability', that is, assumptions that the mother is always responsible for her child, and that her absence – when, for example, she is at work – deprives her children of mothering, which presumably leads to their development being deeply flawed (Macdonald, 2010: 21). These ideologies, held and reproduced by both mothers and nannies in a US context, make the practice of paid care into a terrain of control, MacDonald argued, resulting in different attempts at 'mothering by proxy'. It makes the nanny into a 'shadow mother': an extension of the mother, with no possibility of being an autonomous agent of her own, who should do care just as the mother would have done it, had she been present, and then vanish as soon as the 'real' mother returns (MacDonald, 2010: 110).

The Swedish parents in our study seem less concerned with and affected by ideologies of mother–child bonds and the need for mothers to be physically present in everyday care. While different expectations of mothers and fathers still prevail, and while some mothers – but also some fathers – express concern about their absence, leaving children in the care of others has a long history in Sweden given the prevalence of daycare centres. Still, our study shows that the hiring of nannies and au pairs affords parents other opportunities to orchestrate the care situation, as compared to, for example, public daycare[1]; this difference is visible in the lists delineating tasks and the instructions regarding the activities nannies should do with the children. In addition, many parents have expectations for the nanny and the au pair to fulfil, including the realisation of 'ideal' ways to be with children, for example, serving healthy food or enforcing strict rules for the use of electronic devices, ideals that the parents themselves – at least according to the nannies and au pairs – do not always live up to.

In addition, as we have seen throughout the book, orchestration is often implicit as a lot of the expectations of a 'good' nanny/au pair are unspoken. She should just 'know' what to do in certain situations, and since she is expected to be close to the children and offer them her full attention, she is more 'child-centred' than what is the case with the staff in daycare centres, where many children share the attention of a few caregivers. In this way, she is doing 'intensive parenting' by proxy by fulfilling the ideal of an 'emotionally absorbing' relationship. Elements of both 'puppeteering' and 'paranormal' parenting – detailed steering and expectations of her 'just knowing' (MacDonald, 2010: 90f) – are also present in the Swedish parents' orchestrating, both of which leave little room for the nanny's/au pair's own knowledge of what would be a good way of handling a care situation. It is in this light that we should interpret the substantial amount of energy that nannies and au pairs spend on 'figuring out' what parents expect of them, and also sometimes their use of deception: doing what they think is right when in the care situation, while presenting the parents with an image corresponding with the parents' expectations.[2]

However, at the same time, hiring nannies and au pairs also has elements of withdrawal. In his study of an upper-class neighbourhood in Sweden, Mikael Holmqvist (2015) argued that detached parenting has been an ideal practice within this societal group for a long time. Involvement in 'the grey everyday, with all its trivial concerns and troubles', is to be avoided as a parent, he argued, as doing 'dirty work' does not correspond well with an upper-class lifestyle of 'status' and 'independence' (Holmqvist, 2015: 391, our translation). In our study, detachment from the tedium of daily life seems less connected to 'upper-class' ideals and more connected to ideals of having certain kinds of careers: the working life described by the parents requires long hours away, full focus on work and the possibility of being flexible. To enter this game is incoherent with involvement in mundane everyday care, in the parents' view. This retreat from (some) care can also be part of parenting, as visible in Filippa's feminist statement that she, through her lifestyle, demonstrates to her children that mothers are not just 'caring', but also capable of having careers. However, more importantly, absenting oneself from the dirty work turns parenting into a practice taking place in and through 'good times': not only do couples fight less, but so too do parents and children.

This prompts us to ask: how is parenting transformed when the hardship of the everyday is removed? What happens when the 'dirty work' is extracted and replaced by 'quality time' together? It is a compelling image that is painted by the parents, of a parent–child relationship relieved of both hard physical work, the stress of handling the unexpected and negative emotions associated with 'musts' and 'nagging'. However, our study shows that, while being understanding and appreciative of the good things that the parents' demanding work situation brings to the family, and while being positive towards the relationships they develop with their nannies and au pairs in many cases, children still wish for more of an engagement of their parents in the everyday mundane care situation. This image is supported in Christensen's study of children and time, where she shows that children's ideas of 'quality time' and 'family time' diverges from parents': children value the ordinariness and routine of mundane everyday 'simple' activities such as watching television together or sharing a meal. Also, the significance of knowing that someone is there for you, when and if you need them, cannot be scheduled, Christensen argues, but is intertwined in the everyday doings. In addition, children put great value in having a say over their time, of having the possibility to decide when to spend time with others, when to be alone and when to have peace and quiet. Interestingly, the children in Christensen's study do not see everyday conflicts and disputes as necessarily problematic, but rather as something to be expected in everyday interactions (Christensen, 2002: 81–7).

The children in our study – like all children in Sweden – are used to spending time away from their parents, and they are used to experiencing care situations with carers other than their mothers and fathers. Our argument is not that of 'blanket accountability' mothering or parenting, which inevitably ends up in conservative – and often gender-conservative – arguments that 'mothers/parents always know best' and should be the ones staying at home with their children. However, ideals of stress- and conflict-free parenting are built on assumptions that go against children's own accounts of what is important to them. It is in the mundane everyday interactions of care that relationships are made. When care instead becomes an involvement of only positive emotions and doings in 'good times', it is likely to change the character of relationships. While the parents' wish for less conflict and more 'quality time' is very understandable, there are reasons to critically investigate how this is transforming relationships between parents and children more generally.

The ideals of stress-free parenting, as well as the importance of having 'quality time' with one's children, are not limited to this group of parents; on the contrary, it seems to be a reoccurring and increasingly widespread ideal among different groups of parents (Christensen, 2002; Cardell, 2015; Alsarve et al, 2017). However, the solution to the jigsaw puzzle of life suggested by the parents in this study is not available to everyone. Intensive mothering/parenting is inherently classed (Lareau, 2003; Macdonald, 2010): while presenting itself as a generally 'publicly accepted version of contemporary good parenting', it is a middle-class ideal that requires certain economic means to fulfil (Dermott and Pomati, 2015: 2–3; see also Gillies, 2010). Our study prompts us to ask whether the same classed dimensions are at work when considering the stress-free family and parenting ideal. To be able to create this 'quality time' of parenting, relieved from mundane everyday care responsibilities – and conflicts – while simultaneously solving the jigsaw puzzle of life without compromising one's career, financial means are necessary. The mundane everyday care chores still need to be done by someone, and the new possibilities for Swedish families – state supported as they are – of buying domestic services in the form of nannies and au pairs can thereby be argued to make both gender equality and stress-free parenting into ideals that can only possibly be achieved by some.

Transforming the Swedish welfare state: reformulating equality

Returning to where we started: is it still accurate to describe Sweden as a 'caring state', as Norwegian sociologist Arnlaug Leira (1994) argued in the mid-1990s? The idea of providing good care for all came out of an ideal of social as well as gender equality, as in the dual-earner/dual-carer ideal, with the aim of making it possible for women and men of all social classes to work outside of the home and have their children in affordable, high-quality public daycare, and to share the remaining part of the care work between themselves. However, the political initiatives of the last decade attest to a change of scenery. The introduction of the RUT tax deduction on household services in 2007 was a reform in the policy area of *taxes*, not in family politics. However, as we have shown throughout this book, it did affect the doings of family.

Even in the preparatory works for the tax deduction, the emphasis was primarily put on the employers, with the underlying assumption that the careers and the care/family dilemma of *some* men and women, namely, those with financial means, was more important than others. This attests to a transformed meaning of gender equality: it was obviously no longer *for all*. Thereby, in effect, the tax deduction led to a breach of the ideal of *social* equality: domestic service was intended for some to use, and for others to perform, making gender equality into a privilege (see also Kvist and Petersen, 2010; Gavanas and Calleman, 2013; Carbin et al, 2017).

Assumptions about who is most fitting to do this kind of work are explicitly marked by class and ethnicity in the policy arena: the RUT tax deduction aimed to create jobs for 'poorly educated persons and groups with low employment opportunities, such as immigrant women, and provide them with a gateway to the labour-market' (Kvist and Peterson, 2010: 193). In this sense, history is repeating itself: in post-war Sweden, poor German girls were seen as particularly suited to be maids, when young and rural working-class Swedish girls found other occupations in the booming economy (Strollo, 2013). As labour law scholar Catharina Calleman (2011: 122) has argued, whenever there are other possibilities, domestic work is rejected. However, and contrary to studies of domestic work in other contexts (Anderson, 2000; Rivas, 2002), the parents in our study very rarely talked explicitly about class and ethnicity. In the few instances when this occurred, it was in disidentificatory terms, for example, contrasting one's own practice of hiring au pairs to that of the ones hiring 'Filipinas' (implicitly assuming that these girls are more commonly exploited), or in appreciatory terms, for example, referring to German girls as especially 'trustworthy', or framing a nanny's or an au pair's working-class background as enriching for the child, who gets to meet different kinds of people. As in the case of gender, as noted in Chapter 6, ethnicity and class seems to form a silent background, for which there is no appropriate language (Frankenberg, 1993; Lilja, 2015). The class and ethnicity of those who do family through hiring nannies and au pairs, and those who make this doing of family possible, is a background condition that, while acknowledged in public policy, is remarkably invisible in the everyday framing of the practice.

Important to note, however, is that the growing private market for domestic care services in Sweden cannot be seen as a serious challenge to the publicly organised daycare system. Since the beginning of the 1990s, Swedish parents have had increased opportunities to choose among different daycare providers, public as well as private (Brennan et al, 2012). While this can be seen as a part of the discourse of 'parents' right to choose', neither this change nor the tax deduction on household services has led to a shift away from daycare (public and private) to paid domestic care only. Still, it has affected the ideal of what *parenting* should be. The growing market of privately employed nannies and au pairs creates a possibility for those who can afford it to do 'good' parenting in new ways. This group's achievement of living up to the ideal, in turn, creates a moral narrative of 'stress-free' quality-time parenting where the financial backdrop is obscured.

Leira's (1994) identification of Sweden as a 'caring state' is, in some respects, still true: family politics continuously stresses gender equality as a shared earner and carer ideal, as visible in, for example, the 'daddy quota', and social equality is strived for through initiatives such as low fees for daycare. However, changes in other policy areas not commonly thought of as regulating family life are reproducing inequalities between families. The tax policy of RUT has enabled the doing of 'good gender-equal families' for some, based on an invisible doing of family by domestic workers, reproducing inequalities of gender, class and ethnicity. It has enabled a vast and growing market for domestic services to emerge in the midst of welfare state Sweden, and, in doing so, it has also created a discursive change, where buying such services is a legitimate way of solving the 'jigsaw puzzle of life'.

The future of the nanny and au pair markets

The number of nannies and au pairs does not seem to be decreasing, rather the opposite. In the last couple of years, the market has also taken a somewhat different turn. In 2014, when we carried out the interviews with Swedish nanny companies, almost all of them stated that they did not want to provide both nanny and cleaning services. Instead, they claimed that they wanted to focus on the nanny market solely, and explicitly emphasised the importance of separating the two in order to 'professionalise' the nanny occupation to be about caring for children. Today, in 2018, several companies' web pages claim that they now offer both nanny services and cleaning services, and that these can often be performed by the same person (see Dagens Industri, 2017). While this could be seen as a way for the companies to make more money by engaging in different areas of household work, it could also be seen as a definite end of what was once called 'the maid debate'. Having someone employed to clean your house and take care of your children is no longer viewed as something exceptional, and scandals of the kind that were witnessed ten years ago are unlikely: opposition to the existence of a domestic services market is diminished, and few political actors raise concern today over this being a sign of the re-emergence of a class society of 'masters and maids' (Kvist, 2013: 215).

The future of the au pair market is somewhat more difficult to foresee. As noted in the introduction, the majority of au pairs are invisible as intra-European Union (EU) au pairs are not visible in the statistics. Therefore, indications of increases or decreases are, by nature, speculative. However, in the light of the more general increase in the acceptance of privately outsourced care, there are reasons to believe that the number of au pairs will not diminish.

The recent development in neighbouring Denmark also attests to the contingency of the market. During the last couple of years, Denmark has had a very active au pair association (organised by the Danish Workers Union), primarily targeting au pairs from the Philippines. They have, among other things, won a number of legal cases against employers who have mistreated their employees, and these have received extensive media interest, making the use and misuse of au pairs visible (Liversage et al, 2013). This, in turn, has led to reforms in au pair regulations in Denmark, increasing the au pairs' salaries, as well as putting demands on employing families to provide weekly schedules and pay for travel costs and insurance. Simultaneously, a decrease in the number of au pair work permits has occurred. On the one hand, this decline could be a sign of an actual decrease in the number of au pairs in Denmark. On the other hand, a more probable explanation is that this is an indication of parents being unwilling to adjust to the stricter rules and to pay more for having an au pair, and, as a consequence, increasingly turning towards the informal market (Avisen, 2017). Another possible explanation lies in a shift in the category of au pairs being hired, that is, that the previously dominant and visible category of Filipina (and other non-EU) au pairs – workers who require work permits – is being replaced by European au pairs, who, as in the case of Sweden, are not visible in any statistics.

In contrast to Denmark, there has been very little interest in the situation of au pairs in Sweden, either in political debates or from unions. In our contacts with labour unions, the reason for this has been motivated by the low number of workers within this category. This points to an inherent problem for this group: as the official statistics only capture some actors within the group, precarious working situations for the majority of au pairs – the ones on the informal market, as well as the intra-EU au pairs – are unlikely to get the interest of unions.

Looking back, we are reminded of how history repeats itself. Ever since the early 20th century, domestic workers' rights have been disregarded in favour of employers. Their rights have always been weaker, something that was historically motivated by the work being performed within other people's homes, and the legislation mainly aimed to protect the employer's privacy. While there have been changes for the better, the employer's perspective has remained the dominant one (Calleman, 2011). The idea in the 1970s, when the Domestic Work Act was last reformed, was that this form of work should soon be superseded by public care services. However, recent developments attest to the opposite: the market is growing, leaving a growing number of workers in jobs regulated by outdated labour laws and vague regulations.

In Sweden, nannies as well as au pairs are considered as workers (though the regulations considering au pairs are contradictory), but they are still regarded as *another kind of worker*: their rights are still not the same as other workers' and there is no union organising them. The working conditions of nannies and au pairs differ in terms of class, migratory position and position on the labour market, but what they all share is an engagement in an activity that is labelled in very misleading ways that do not correspond with the actual practice of doing care. As long as the point of departure is that care is easy work that can easily be delegated, it is likely that the work situation for those involved will continue to be disregarded and precarious.

Good care?

The most common question that we have been asked while carrying out this project is, 'So, is nanny and au pair care good or bad for children, then?'. Discourses of what is 'best for children' always involve moral – and sometimes moralistic – assumptions and arguments. Too often, underlying the whole pursuit of claiming to know 'what is best for children' lie assumptions through which the person arguing is trying to proclaim a particular, personally held, world view, not always related to children per se. Children are used as bats in fights over political agendas, and especially so regarding issues related to care and parenting. Claiming to know 'what is best for children' is often an effective tool in the sense that it often trumps everything else: for a parent to take a certain action – like moving to a safer area or town, placing a child in the best school, or providing a child with the possibility of learning English through an au pair – in the name of 'this is what is best for my child' is enough of an argument to excuse the fact that the practice might be reproducing inequalities between different groups of children.

What is often lacking in all these arguments, and what is probably also the reason why adults so easily take on the role of representing children, is that children are rarely given the opportunity to be heard on matters themselves. However, even when children are listened to, representation – for example, in research – is an especially difficult matter because of children's overall subservient status in society (James, 2007; Komulainen, 2007; Eldén, 2013a). Childhood researchers are by no means exempt from adult-centrism and the temptations of presenting a unified 'truth' about what children really say on matters (Spyrou, 2011). As is the case in all research, our representations are always contingent and need to be critically reassessed over time. However, that said, we do argue that interviewing children about their experience of having nannies and au pairs care for them in their everyday lives has contributed new and very important insights into the practice as such. Children's narratives about care situations enabled us to capture the full complexity of care in everyday life and to get a new understanding of nanny and au pair care.

The children in our study also provide their views on whether nanny and au pair care is good, and as with most adult subjects, when asked about a specific matter, they have different opinions: some like their nannies and au pairs; some dislike them; some see the advantages of having a nanny or an au pair; and some stress the downsides. Several hold all these attitudes at the same time, pointing to the 'messiness' that is inherent in care (Eldén, 2013a). Thus, to answer the question whether this is 'good care', we need to rephrase it and instead ask: what circumstances seem to be necessary for good care to be possible?

Our interviews with children give rather uniform answers to this question: for the children, good care is experienced in situations where nannies and au pairs *engage*, and to do that is to do more than their designated chores – to be ready to take on everything that the specific care situation requires. This necessitates sentient activity on the part of the nannies and au pairs, as we argued in Chapter 6, and, indeed, as care is always relational, children also need to engage in sentient activity. When this happens, care is good in the eyes of children. Close and specific relationships can develop, characterised by feelings not only of love, but of the whole array of emotions that caring relationships entail, and emotional doings that prove this relationship, such as 'knowing' and 'tuning in' to each other, and then being prepared – and having the possible means – to act upon this knowledge. At the same time, the children's narratives also show us that this is not always happening; not all nannies and au pairs engage. In addition, children can and do also express resistance towards being in care situations, especially so after having experienced several turns in the 'nanny circle'. What becomes apparent, then, is that the surrounding framework of constant break-ups and expectations of engaging in new care situations with new nannies and au pairs is not working well with the actual practices that the care situations require.

This image is supported by the narratives shared with us by nannies and au pairs. While previous studies have pointed to the way in which structural circumstances outside of family relations put nannies and au pairs in precarious positions, our study points to the necessity of also taking into account the ways in which *understandings of care in families* make the situation precarious. The gap between expectations and experiences identified in Chapter 6 showed that the organisation of care through nannies and au pairs does not take into account the fundamental character of care as sentient activity.

Indeed, this is not only the case for paid care taking place in private settings; as studies of caregivers within publicly organised care facilities show, these workers experience similar problems of gaps between the experience of being in care situations and the expectations of the role of caregiver (Nelson, 1989; Murray, 1998; Lydahl, 2017). As long as care is either understood within frameworks of 'naturalness' and female intuition or reduced to being only about 'labour', in the logic of 'scientification' (Wærness, 1984: 190), this gap will remain. What we are calling for is a return to the critical discussion of the 1980s and 1990s, where theorising of care moved beyond the dichotomy of labour and emotion and pointed to the structural inequalities being created in and through care practices. This will enable a discussion of care that takes as its point of departure the full complexity of the practice, and only through this can forms of doing care – both unpaid and paid care activities, and care activities outside and inside the private sphere – be fully understood. While pointing to the similarities of caregiving experiences outside of and inside 'the family', this discussion also needs to take into consideration differences between settings: the organisation of, for example, care in public daycare facilities differs in important respects from the framework for doing paid care in families. As Mason (1996) argues, a too general theory of care will fail to acknowledge the specific ways in which care is done within family and kinship relations, and how this doing is constitutive of 'family'. This is, as we have shown throughout this book, especially the case when care is done by a paid care worker: the invisible glue that keeps the jigsaw puzzle of life from falling apart will stay invisible – and precarious – unless all of her complex doings of care are acknowledged. As long as this is not happening, there are strong reasons to believe that 'good care' – that is, a care situation that recognises the needs and conditions of all parties involved – is difficult to realise.

Notes

Chapter 1

[1] It is however questionable whether the rules were followed in Reinfeldt's case as au pairs from outside the European Union (EU) (which was the case here) are regulated by two contradictory rules: the work permit requirements and the Domestic Work Act (discussed in Anving and Eldén, 2016).

[2] Bill 2006/07, no. 94, 'Skattelättnader för hushållstjänster, m.m.' ['Tax deductions for domestic services, etc.'], https://data.riksdagen.se/fil/86622E56-6141-4B1F-A1C3-C8B462AFD3CF

[3] The term 'jigsaw puzzle of life' was introduced by the TCO union in 2002 (Swedish Confederation of Professional Employees) and is widely used in political debate on the work–family balance.

[4] The tendency to describe gender equality as a part of 'Swedishness' has been highly, and rightly, criticised by, particularly, post-colonial feminists, arguing that differences between different men and women have been neglected and that gender equality has been portrayed as something that is inhabited by Swedes. This, as a consequence, distinguished an imagined 'us' from 'them', described as inhabiting less modern and familial ideals (see, for example, Wikström, 2007; Mulinari, 2009).

[5] This was also the case in elderly care, as well as within the school system (see, for example, Ulmanen and Szebehely, 2015; Bunar and Sernhede, 2013; Ulmanen, 2015).

[6] RUT is an acronym for 'Rengöring, Underhåll, Tvätt' ('Cleaning, Maintenance, Laundry').

[7] When the Social Democrats and the Green Party came to power in 2014, they kept the deduction but lowered the amount that could be deducted. In 2018, it was possible to make a tax deduction for cleaning, nanny services, some gardening work, the installation of information technology (IT) equipment and the renovation of white goods (Swedish Tax Agency, 2018). The RUT tax deduction continues to be high on the political agenda, with suggestions from several political parties of expanding it further.

[8] See Bill 2006/07, no. 94, 'Skattelättnader för hushållstjänster, m.m.' ['Tax deductions for domestic services, etc.'], https://data.riksdagen.se/fil/86622E56-6141-4B1F-A1C3-C8B462AFD3CF

[9] There is also an informal market, but this is not in focus for this study. We have, however, met with nannies who worked both formally and informally in different families at the same time, and also with parents who have hired nannies and au pairs both formally and informally.

[10] This was reported in interviews with nanny agencies.

11 Costs and salaries are from 2014 when we performed interviews with nanny agencies. The numbers for 2018 are somewhat higher.

12 Around 2,400 au pair work/residence permits were issued in Denmark in 2011 (Liversage et al, 2013), compared to 1,500 in 2004 (Stenum, 2010), mainly issued to au pairs from the Philippines. In Norway, 158 au pair visas were issued in 1994, compared to 1,500 in 2013 (86 per cent to au pairs from the Philippines), but the total number, including au pairs from the EU, is probably twice as high (Stubberud, 2015). Au pair work permits have decreased in Denmark over the last few years due to stricter rules for employing au pairs, but, at the same time, it is likely that this has resulted in an increase in intra-EU au pairs who are – as in the case of Sweden – not visible in statistics (Avisen, 2017).

13 In some cases, our study attests that the parents instead tried to get them enrolled in Swedish for Immigrants (SFI), which is free of charge.

14 Despite the Migration Agency regulations, the work conditions of au pairs coming from outside of the EU are also, in theory, regulated by the Domestic Work Act. This means that all au pairs in Sweden are legally considered as workers, a fact that very few actors involved are aware of (these contradictions are discussed in detail in Anving and Eldén, 2016).

Chapter 2

1 Sentient activity, Mason argues, is conceptualised in combination with *active sensibility*, 'the activity of feeling responsibility for someone, or a commitment to someone else', which involves 'taking a responsibility on board as something which is your own' (Mason, 1996: 31).

2 In many respects, the specificity of Souralová's case sets hers apart from the majority of studies in the global care chain research field as the nannies are natives, of old age and often confident in their caring role, contrary to the parents, being immigrants and hardly involved in the care situation at all (Souralová, 2013: 143–4). Also, Souralová's study consists of retrospective narratives, through interviews with now adult children.

3 Several global care chain scholars do, indeed, acknowledge the difficulties involved in using the labour–love dichotomy, but there are still few other options presented (see, for example, Yeates, 2012: 151–2).

4 The study was funded by the *Swedish Foundation for Humanities and Social Sciences* (Eldén P13-0603:1).

5 This could possibly be explained by previous media exposure due to cases of sexual harassment towards au pairs (Calleman, 2010).

6 The majority of parents and au pairs in our sample had made use of web platforms, for example, AupairWorld.com or Facebook, although some had experience of using au pair agencies.

7 At one point, we were in contact with a group of au pairs that we knew were in a very precarious position, but they withdrew at the very last minute.

8 In addition, it was often difficult to find a time when the parents could meet with us, and, in some cases, they also made clear that their time was limited. Similar experiences of access/non-access were reported by Macdonald (2010) in her study of employer mothers and their nannies and au pairs. Researchers focusing on privileged groups (to which one could argue many of the parents in this study belong) often point to this group's unwillingness to participate in research (Nader,

1979; Holmqvist, 2018; Sohl, 2018). However, it is important to note that some parents participating in the study were also genuinely interested and helpful, and were very interested in the research and our upcoming results.

[9] We have also interviewed (in person or via telephone) representatives from nanny agencies (six), au pair agencies (two), churches organising au pair activities (three), the Swedish Migration Agency and the Swedish Tax Agency. In addition, we collected and analysed different documents stating the rules for au pair work in Sweden, both information from authorities (the Tax Agency and the Migration Agency) and legal documents (the Domestic Work Act), as well as information given on au pair agency websites.

[10] While there are occasionally men posting adverts on au pair sites, and some nanny companies have men employed, although primarily as tutors, the market is very female dominated. This is also reflected in the parent interviews: of the 83 nannies and au pairs hired by families in this study, all were women.

[11] To employ students was an explicit strategy on the part of the nanny agencies. All agencies that we interviewed said that their main target group, and most preferred employees, were Swedish-speaking students since they were most sought after by their customers.

[12] All except one had au pair work permits; one girl had only obtained a tourist visa.

[13] The interviews with the nannies and au pairs were mostly conducted in a cafe. No nanny or au pair chose to meet us in their employer's home.

[14] Initially, we had also planned to do diary interviews with parents, but since only a few completed their diary, they did not play an important part in the semi-structured interviews that we ended up performing. The parents chose a place to meet; in most cases, we visited in their homes, while some interviews were performed at the parent's workplace or in a cafe.

[15] This work was carried out by a professional transcription company.

[16] Ethical Review Board, Lund Sweden (Eldén 2014/94).

[17] In a couple of cases, parents that we had interviewed did, in fact, put us in contact with their nannies and au pairs. In these cases, we were extra careful when contacting the nanny/au pair to not put pressure on her to participate.

[18] Informed consent was obtained in writing from all adult participants. Regarding children, written consent was obtained from legal guardians, and verbal consent from children (Eldén, 2013b), following the ethical guidelines of the Swedish Research Council (VR, 2017).

Chapter 3

[1] The interviews in this study have been carried out in Swedish and English, and the Swedish quotes have been translated by the authors.

[2] In the quoted interview material in this book, ellipses are enclosed in square brackets while pauses in speech are not.

[3] One mother decided against hiring an au pair and sticking to nannies as she figured that their time with the children was more limited and would not compete with her position as the primary person in the lives of her children. For another, the closeness that did, indeed, develop between her children and the au pair was the reason to prematurely end the contract.

Chapter 4

[1] In a few cases, the au pairs had made use of an au pair agency when coming to Sweden. Some reflected upon the possibility of talking to them if a problematic situation arouse but said that they would be reluctant to do so.

[2] There are also nannies working informally, and some of the nannies in our study worked both in the formal and informal sector. However, the formally employed nannies were the point of departure for this study.

[3] Enduring harsh conditions has been described by other researchers as 'a rite of passage' of au pairing: a transient stage between high school and university and a trial that young girls taking placements as au pairs feel that they have to pass, no matter how oppressive the work conditions are, in order to come out as grown-ups (Búriková and Miller, 2010). While this might be the case for some au pairs in our study too, the primary reasons for staying with the family despite difficult conditions has rather to do with a lack of other opportunities.

[4] Búriková (2015) discusses the importance of informal social networks and argues that gossip plays a significant role when au pairs try to find out about the rules and norms of au pairing, and situate themselves in relation to these. Similar tendencies are visible in our study as au pairs talk about frequently engaging in discussions and comparisons of working conditions, both offline and online (primarily in Facebook groups) (Dalgas, 2016). Nannies also compare working conditions, but despite the fact that they are employed by an agency, they rarely meet. Some agencies organise courses and meetings, but not all nannies attend. Thus, both groups are relatively isolated and highly dependent on their own abilities to form and sustain informal networks (Sassen, 2002).

Chapter 5

[1] We could not detect any differences between how girls and boys perceived of and related to nannies and au pairs. As our examples in this chapter show, both boys and girls developed close relationships to nannies and au pairs, and both categories could also express and talk about reluctance and distance. While gender is thoroughly theorised about from the perspective of care providers (as being female), the significance of the gender of care 'receivers', especially in relation to children and the elderly, is not problematised to the same extent (Wærness, 1984).

Chapter 6

[1] This is not an enterprise taken on only by the employing party; studies of childcare workers in family care and daycare settings attest to employees also using the vocabulary of being 'like wives' and 'like mum' (Nelson, 1989; Murray, 1998; Macdonald, 2010; O'Connell, 2010). The nannies and au pairs in our study also position themselves in these terms, but, in addition, more gender-neutral nouns are used, such as 'extra parent'.

[2] A representative of a nanny company that we interviewed talked about young men being recruited, but primarily in the role of tutors, which was a service that the company offered at the time.

[3] In this sense, the nanny/au pair role contains simultaneously ambivalence and ambiguity, in the sociological sense of the terms. It reproduces the opposing normative tendencies inherent in traditional female family roles (ambivalence),

while, at the same time, being ambiguous as the role is not 'secure or well defined' (Luescher and Pillemer, 1998: 416–17).

Chapter 7

[1] These institutions are regulated and controlled by curricula set by the Swedish National Agency for Education.

[2] In a more general sense, the nannies and au pairs are making possible 'activity-intensive' quality time for the children (Demott and Pomati, 2015) – one of the major tasks of nannies and au pairs being to take the children to their many afternoon activities – without the parents having to compromise their own time at work. The hiring of nannies and au pairs can, in this sense, be seen as intensive parenting by proxy, enabling the parents to be part of the larger 'culture of intensive parenting in which parents are expected to engage in a range of child-centred activities on a regular basis' (Demott and Pomati, 2015: 14; see also Faircloth and Lee, 2010), without necessarily being physically present themselves.

References

Aarseth, H. (2014) 'Finanskapitalismens kjønns-romantikk: Næringslivselitens kjønnskomplmentære familiekultur' ['The gender romance of finance capitalism: Gender complementary in business elite families'], *Tidskrift for kjønnsforskning*, 38(3/4): 203–18.

Ahlberg, J., Roman, C. and Duncan, S. (2008) 'Actualizing the "democratic family"?: Swedish policy rhetoric versus family practices', *Social Politics*, 15: 79–100.

Alsarve, J., Lundqvist, Å. and Roman, C. (2017) *Ensamma mammor: Dilemman, resurser, strategier* [*Lone mothers. Dilemmas, resources and strategies*], Malmö: Gleerups.

Anderson, B. (2000) *Doing the dirty work? The global politics of domestic labour*, London: Zed Books.

Anving, T. (2012) *Måltidens paradoxe. Om klass och kön i vardagens familjepraktiker* [*Meal paradoxes. Class and gender in everyday family practices*], Lund: Lund University.

Anving, T. and Eldén, S. (2016) 'Precarious care labor: Contradictory work regulations and practices for au pairs in Sweden', *Nordic Journal of Working Life Studies*, 6(4): 29–48.

Avisen (2017) 'Nye tal: Rekordfå danske familier hyrer au pair-piger' ['New numbers: Very few Danish families hire au pairs'], www.avisen. dk/nye-tal-flere-danske-familier-dropper-billige-filip_452208.aspx

Becker, H.S. (1998) *Tricks of the trade: How to think about your research while you're doing it*, Chicago, IL: University of Chicago Press.

Bikova, M. (2017) *The egalitarian hear: Glocal care chains in the Filipino au pair migration to Norway*, Bergen: University of Bergen.

Björnberg, U. (2002) 'Work and care of children: Family policies and balancing work and family in Sweden', in A. Carling, S. Duncan and R. Edwards (eds) *Analysing families: Morality and rationality in Policy and Practice*, London: Routledge.

Bjørnholt, M. and Farstad, G.R. (2014) '"Am I rambling?": On the advantages of interviewing couples together', *Qualitative Research*, 14(3): 3–19.

Bolger, N., Davis, A. and Rafaeli, E. (2003) 'Diary methods: Capturing life as it is lived', *Annual Review of Psychology*, 54(1): 579–616.

Borchorst, A. and Siim, B. (2008) 'Woman-friendly policies and state feminism', *Feminist Theory*, 9: 207–24.

Boye, K., Halldén, K. and Magnusson, C. (2014) 'Könslönegapets utveckling: Betydelsen av yrkets kvalifikationsnivå och familjeansvar' ['The gender pay gap: The significance of qualification level and family responsibility], in M. Evertsson and C. Magnusson (eds) *Ojämlikhetens dimensioner: Uppväxtvillkor, arbete och hälsa i Sverige* [*Dimensions of inequalities: Childrearing, work and health in Sweden*], Stockholm: Liber, pp 185–211.

Brannen, J. (2015) *Fathers and sons: Generations, families and migration*, Basingstoke: Palgrave.

Brannen, J. and Heptinstall, E. (2003) 'Concepts of care and children's contribution to family life', in J. Brannen and P. Moss (eds) *Rethinking children's care*, Buckingham: Open University Press, pp 183–97.

Brannen, J., Heptinstall, E. and Bhopal, K. (2000) *Connecting children: Care and family life in later childhood*, London: Routledge.

Brennan, D., Cass, B., Himmelweit, S. and Szebehely, M. (2012) 'The marketisation of care: Rationales and consequences in Nordic and liberal care regimes', *Journal of European Social Policy*, 22(4): 377–91.

Bunar, N. and Sernhede, O. (2013) *Skolan och ojämlikhetens urbana geografi* [*School and the urban geography of inequality*], Göteborg: Daidalos.

Búriková, Z. (2015) '"Good families" and the shadows of servitude: Au pair gossip and norms of au pair employment', in R. Cox (ed) *Au pairs' lives in global context. Sisters or servants?*, Basingstoke: Palgrave Macmillan, pp 36–52.

Búriková, Z. and Miller, D. (2010) *Au pair*, Cambridge: Polity Press.

Calleman, C. (2010) 'Cultural exchange or cheap domestic labour? Constructions of "au pair" in four Nordic countries', in L. Widding Isaksen (ed) *Global care work: Gender and migration in Nordic societies*, Lund: Nordic Academic Press, pp 69–96.

Calleman, C. (2011) 'Domestic services in a land of equality: The case of Sweden', *Canadian Journal of Women and the Law*, 23(1): 121–39.

Carbin, M., Overud, J. and Kvist, E. (2017) *Feminism som lönearbete: Om den svenska arbetslinjen och kvinnors frigörelse* [*Feminism and paid work: Swedish labour politics and women's emancipation*], Stockholm: Leopard Förlag.

Cardell, D. (2015) *Family theme parks, happiness and children's consumption: From roller-coasters to Pippi Longstocking*, Linköping: Linköping University.

Chan, A.H. (2005) 'Live-in foreign domestic workers and their impact on Hong Kong's middle class families', *Journal of Family and Economic Issues*, 26(4): 509–28.

Christensen, P. (2002) 'Why more "quality time" is not on the top of children's lists: The "qualities of time" for children', *Children & Society*, 16(2): 77–88.

Christensen, P. and James, A. (eds) (2008) *Research with children: Perspectives and practices*, London: Routledge.

Constable, N. (2002) 'Filipina workers in Hong Kong homes: Household rules and relations', in B. Ehrenreich and A.R. Hochschild (eds) *Global woman: Nannies, maids, and sex workers in the new economy*, London: Granta Books, pp 115–41.

Corsaro, W. (2015) *The sociology of childhood* (4th edn), Los Angeles, CA: Sage.

Cox, R. (2006) *The servant problem: Domestic employment in a global economy*, London: I.B. Tauris.

Cox, R. (ed) (2015) *Au pairs' lives in global context. Sisters or servants?*, Basingstoke: Palgrave Macmillan.

Dagens Industri (2017) 'Barnpassare tar nya vägar' ['New directions for nannies'], https://weekend.di.se/nyheter/barnpassare-tar-nya-vagar

Dalgas, K.M. (2015) 'Becoming independent through au pair migration: Self-making and social re-positioning among young Filipinas in Denmark', *Identities: Global Studies in Culture and Power*, 22(3): 222–46.

Dalgas, K.M. (2016) 'Au pairs on Facebook: Ethnographic use of social media on politicised fields', *Nordic Journal of Migration Research*, 6(3): 175–82.

Daly, K.J. (1996) *Families & time: Keeping pace in a hurried culture*, Thousand Oaks, CA: Sage Publications.

Daly, M. (2013) 'Parenting support: Another gender-related policy illusion in Europe?', *Women's Studies International Forum*, 41(2013): 223–30.

Davies, H.M. (2011) 'Sharing surnames: Children, family and kinship', *Sociology*, 45(4): 554–69.

Davies, H.M. (2015) *Understanding children's personal lives and relationships*, Basingstoke: Palgrave Macmillan.

Dermott, E. and Seymour, J. (eds) (2011) *Displaying families: A new concept for the sociology of family life*, Basingstoke: Palgrave Macmillan.

Dermott, E. and Pomati, M. (2015) '"Good" parenting practices: How important are poverty, education and time pressure?', *Sociology*, 50(1): 125–42.

DeVault, M.L. (1991) *Feeding the family: The social organization of caring as gendered work*, Chicago, IL: University of Chicago Press.

Ehrenreich, B. and Hochschild, A.R. (eds) (2002) *Global woman: Nannies, maids, and sex workers in the new economy*, London: Granta Books.

Eldén, S. (2013a) 'Inviting the messy: Drawing methods and "children's voices"', *Childhood*, 20(1): 66–81.

Eldén, S. (2013b) '"Your child is just wonderful!": On ethics and access in research with children', *Journal of Comparative Social Work*, 2: 1–24.

Eldén, S. (2016) 'An ordinary complexity of care: Moving beyond "the family" in research with children', *Families, Relationships and Societies*, 5(2): 175–92.

Eldén, S. and Anving, T. (2016) 'New ways of doing the "good" and gender equal family: Parents employing nannies and au pairs in Sweden', *Sociological Research Online*, 21(4): 2.

Ellingsaeter, A.L. and Leira, A. (2006) 'Epilogue: Scandinavian policies of parenthood – a success story?', in A.L. Ellingsaeter and A. Leira (eds) *Politicising parenthood in Scandinavia: Gender relations in welfare states*, Bristol: Policy Press, pp 265–77.

Esping-Andersen, G. (1999) *Social foundations of postindustrial economies*, New York, NY: Oxford University Press.

Faircloth, C. and Lee, E. (2010) 'Introduction: Changing parenting culture', *Sociological Research Online*, 15(4): 1.

Finch, J. (2007) 'Displaying families', *Sociology*, 41(1): 65–81.

Finch, J. and Groves, D. (eds) (1983) *A labour of love: Women, work and caring*, London: Routledge & Kegan Paul.

Fink, J. (ed) (2004) *Care: Personal lives and social policy*, Milton Keynes: The Open University.

Frankenberg, R. (1993) *White women, race matters. The social construction of whiteness*, London: Routledge.

Fraser, N. (1994) 'After the family wage: Gender equity and the welfare state', *Political Theory*, 22(4): 591–618.

Gabb, J. (2010) *Researching intimacy in families*, Basingstoke: Palgrave Macmillan.

Gavanas, A. (2010) *Who cleans the welfare state? Migration, informalization, social exclusion and domestic services in Stockholm*, Stockholm: Institute for Futures Studies.

Gavanas, A. (2013) 'Migrant domestic workers, social network strategies and informal markets for domestic services in Sweden', *Women's Studies International Forum*, 36: 56–64.

Gavanas, A. and Calleman, C. (eds) (2013) *Rena hem på smutsiga villkor?: Hushållstjänster, migration och globalisering* [*Clean homes and dirty conditions? Domestic work, migration and globalisation*], Göteborg: Makadam.

Gillies, V. (2010) 'Is poor parenting a class issue? Contextualizing anti-social behaviour and family life', in M. Klett-Davies (ed) *Is parenting a class issue?*, London: Family and Parenting Institute, pp 44–61.

Gillies, V. (2011) 'From function to competence: Engaging in the new politics of "the family"', *Sociological Research Online*, 16(4): 11.

Gilligan, C. (1982) *In a different voice: Psychological theory and women's development*, Cambridge: Harvard University Press.

Graham, H. (1983) 'Caring: A labour of love', in J. Finch and D. Groves (eds) *A labour of love: Women, work and caring*, London: Routledge & Kegan Paul, pp 13–30.

Graham, H. (1991) 'The concept of caring in feminist research: The case of domestic service', *Sociology*, 25(1): 61–78.

Grönlund, A. and Halleröd, B. (eds) (2008) *Jämställdhetens pris* [*The price of gender equality*], Umeå: Boréa.

Gullestad, M. (1984) *Kitchen-table society: A case study of the family life and friendships of young working-class mothers in urban Norway*, Bergen: University of Bergen Press.

Gunnarsson, Å. (2013) 'Introduction', in Å. Gunnarsson (ed) *Tracing the women-friendly welfare state: Gender politics of everyday life in Sweden*, Stockholm: Makadam, pp 9–16.

Halldén, G. (2010) 'Barndomsbegreppet som tidsspegel' ['The concept of childhood as a mirror of time'], in A. Banér (ed) *Barnets familjer ur barnkulturella perspektiv* [*Children's families from a child cultural perspective*], Stockholm: Centre for Childhood Studies, Stockholm University, pp 55–66.

Hays, S. (1996) *The cultural contradictions of motherhood*, New Haven, CT: Yale University Press.

Hernes, H. (1987) *Welfare state and woman power: Essays in state feminism*, London: Norwegian University Press.

Hirdman, Y. (1989) *Att lägga livet till rätta: Studier i svensk folkhemspolitik* [*Putting life to order: Studies of the 'peoples' home' policies in Sweden*], Stockholm: Carlsson.

Hochschild, A.R. (2000) 'Global care chains and emotional surplus value', in W. Hutton and A. Giddens (eds) *On the edge: Living with global capitalism*, London: Jonathan Cape, pp 130–46.

Hochschild, A.R. (2002) 'Love and gold', in B. Ehrenreich and A.R. Hochschild (eds) *Global woman: Nannies, maids, and sex workers in the new economy*, London: Granta Books, pp 15–30.

Hochschild, A.R. and Machung, A. (1989) *The second shift: Working parents and the revolution at home*, New York, NY: Viking.

Holmqvist, M. (2015) *Djursholm: Sveriges ledarsamhälle* [*Djursholm: Leader Communities in Sweden*], Stockholm: Atlantis.

Holmqvist, M. (2018) 'Att studera den ekonomiska eliten: Problem och utmaningar' ('Studying the financial elite: Problems and challenges'), *Sociologisk forskning*, 55(1): 5–22.

Hondagneu-Sotelo, P. (2002) 'Blowups and other unhappy endings', in B. Ehrenreich and A.R. Hochschild (eds) *Global woman: Nannies, maids, and sex workers in the new economy*, London: Granta Books, pp 55–69.

Isaksen, L.W. (2010) 'Introduction: Global care work in Nordic societies', in L.W. Isaksen (ed) *Global care work: Gender and migration in Nordic societies*, Lund: Nordic Academic Press.

James, A. (2007) 'Giving voice to children's voices: Practices and problems, pitfalls and potential', *American Anthropologist*, 109(2): 261–72.

James, A. and James, A.L. (2008) *Key concepts in childhood studies*, Los Angeles, CA: Sage.

Jamieson, L. (1998) *Intimacy: Personal relationships in modern societies*, Oxford: Polity Press.

Johansson, T. (2014) 'Män, familj och föräldraskap' ['Men, family and parenthood'], in S. Dahl (ed) *Män och jämställdhet: Betänkande SOU 2014:6 [Men and gender equality: Report SOU 2014:6]*, Stockholm: Fritze, pp 187–209.

Klinth, R. (2002) *Göra pappa med barn: Den svenska pappapolitiken 1960–95 [Making daddies care: Swedish policy on fathers 1960–95]*, Linköping: University of Linköping.

Klinth, R. and Johansson, T. (2010) *Nya svenska fäder [New Swedish fathers]*, Umeå: Boréa.

Komulainen, S. (2007) 'The ambiguity of the child's "voice" in social research', *Childhood*, 14(1): 11–28.

Kvist, E. (2013) 'A booming market of precarious work: Selling domestic services in women-friendly Sweden', in Å. Gunnarsson (ed) *Tracing the women-friendly welfare state: Gender politics of everyday life in Sweden*, Stockholm: Makadam, pp 214–33.

Kvist, E. and Peterson, E. (2010) 'What has gender equality got to do with it? An analysis of policy debates surrounding domestic services in the welfare states of Spain and Sweden', *Nordic Journal of Feminist and Gender Research*, 18(3): 185–203.

Lareau, A. (2003) *Unequal childhoods: The class, race, and family life*, Berkeley, CA: University of California Press.

Lawler, S. (2005) 'Disgusted subjects: The making of middle-class identities', *The Sociological Review*, 53(3): 429–46.

Leira, A. (1994) 'Concepts of caring: Loving, thinking, and doing', *Social Service Review*, 68(2): 185–201.

Lilja, M. (2015) *'Det bästa för mitt barn': Nyblivna mödrar i den delade staden* [*The best for my child: Mothers with small children in the divided city*], Örebro: Örebro University.

Littmarck, S. (2017) *Barn, föräldrar, välfärdsstat: Den politiska debatten om föräldrautbildning och föräldrastöd 1964–2009* [*Children, parents and the welfare state: The political debate on parent education and parent support 1964–2009*], Linköping: Linköping University.

Liversage, A., Bille, R. and Jakobsen, V. (2013) *Den Danske au-pair ordning: En kvalitativ og kvantitativ undersøgels* [*The Danish au pair order: A qualitative and quantitative analysis*] 13:02, København: SFI – Det Nationale Forskningscenter for Velfærd.

Lorentzi, U. (2011) *Alla andra hämtar tidigt: En undersökning av öppettider och tider för lämning och hämtning på förskolor* [*Everybody else picks up early: A report on opening hours and times for leaving and picking up children at daycare*], Stockholm: Kommunal.

Luescher, K. and Pillemer, K. (1998) 'Intergenerational ambivalence: A new approach to the study of parent–child relations in later life', *Journal of Marriage and the Family*, 60(2): 413–25.

Lundqvist, Å. (2007) *Familjen i den svenska modellen* [*Family in the Swedish model*], Umeå: Boréa.

Lundqvist, Å. (2011) *Family policy paradoxes: Gender equality and labour market regulation in Sweden, 1930–2010*, Bristol: Policy Press.

Lundqvist, Å. (2017) *Transforming gender and family relations: How active labour market policies shaped the dual earner model*, Cheltenham: Edward Elgar Publishing.

Lutz, H. (ed) (2008) *Migration and domestic work: A European perspective on a global theme*, Aldershot: Ashgate.

Lutz, H. (2011) *The new maids: Transnational women and the care economy*, London: Zed.

Lydahl, D. (2017) 'Visible persons, invisible work? Exploring articulation work in the implementation of person-centred care on a hospital ward', *Sociologisk forskning*, 54(3): 163–79.

Macdonald, C.L. (2010) *Shadow mothers: Nannies, au pairs, and the micropolitics of mothering*, Berkeley, CA: University of California Press.

Marschall, A. (2014) 'Who cares for whom? Revisiting the concept of care in the everyday life of post-divorce families', *Childhood*, 21(4): 517–31.

Mason, J. (1996) 'Gender, care and sensibility in family and kin relationships', in J. Holland and L. Atkins (eds) *Sex, sensibility and the gendered body*, London: Macmillan, pp 15–36.

Mason, J. (2006) 'Mixing methods in a qualitatively driven way', *Qualitative Research*, 6(1): 9–25.

Mason, J. and Tipper, B. (2008) 'Being related: How children define and create kinship', *Childhood*, 15(4): 441–60.

May, V. (ed) (2011) *Sociology of personal life*, Basingstoke: Palgrave Macmillan.

Morgan, D.H.J. (1996) *Family connections: An introduction to family studies*, Cambridge: Polity Press.

Morgan, D.H.J. (2011) *Rethinking family practices*, Basingstoke: Palgrave Macmillan.

Morrow, V. (1996) 'Rethinking childhood dependency: Children's contributions to the family economy', *The Sociological Review*, 44(1): 58–77.

Mulinari, D. (2009) 'Den "andra" familjen: Genus, nation och migration' ['The "other" family: Gender, nation and migration'], in J. Fink and Å. Lundqvist (eds) *Välfärd, genus och familj* [*Welfare, gender and family*], Malmö: Liber, pp 201–24.

Murray, S.B. (1998) 'Child-care work: Intimacy in the shadows of family-life', *Qualitative Sociology*, 21(2): 149–68.

Myrdal, A. and Myrdal, G. (1934) *Kris i befolkningsfrågan* [*The population crisis*], Stockholm: Bonnier.

Myrdal, A. and Klein, V. (1957) *Kvinnans två roller* [*Women's two roles*], Stockholm: Tiden.

Nader, L. (1979) 'Up the anthropologist: Perspectives gained from studying up', in D. Hyms (ed) *Reinventing anthropology*, New York, NY: Random House, pp 284–31.

Nanny.nu (2018) 'Om nanny.nu' ['About nanny.nu'], https://nanny.nu/om-nannynu/

Näre, L. (2016) 'Neoliberal citizenship and domestic service in Finland: A return to a servant society?', in B. Gullikstad, G. Kristensen and P. Ringrose (eds) *Paid migrant domestic labour in a changing Europe. Citizenship, gender and diversity*, London: Palgrave Macmillan, pp 31–53.

Näre, L. and Wide, E. (forthcoming) 'Local loops of care in the Helsinki region: A time-economy perspective', *Journal of European Social Policy*.

Nelson, M.K. (1989) 'Negotiating care: Relationships between family daycare providers and mothers', *Feminist Studies*, 15(1): 7–33.

Nilsen, A.C. and Wærdahl, R. (2014) 'Gender differences in Norwegian children's work at home', *Childhood*, 22(1): 53–66.

Nordenmark, M. (2008) 'Bråk och rollkonflikter – jämställdhetens avigsida?' [Quarrels and role conflicts – the flip side of gender equality?], in A. Grönlund and B. Halleröd (eds) *Jämställdhetens pris* [*The price of gender equality*], Umeå: Boréa, pp 111–34.

Öberg, L. (1999) 'Ett socialdemokratiskt dilemma: Från hembiträdesfråga till pigdebatt' ['A social democratic dilemma: From a maid-question to a maid debate'], in C. Florin, L. Sommestad and U. Wikander (eds) *Kvinnor mot kvinnor: Om systerskapets svårigheter* [*Women against women: On the difficulties of sisterhood*], Stockholm: Norstedts Förlag, pp 159–99.

O'Connell, R. (2010) 'How is childminding family like? Family day care, food and the reproduction of identity at the public/private interface', *The Sociological Review*, 58(4): 563–86.

Parreñas, R.S. (2001) *Servants of globalization: Migration and domestic work*, Stanford, CA: Stanford University Press.

Parreñas, R.S. (2005) *Children of global migration: Transnational families and gendered woes*, Stanford, CA: Stanford University Press.

Platzer, E. (2006) 'From public responsibility and back again: The new domestic services in Sweden', *Gender & History*, 18: 211–21.

Platzer, E. (2007) *Från folkhem till karriärhushåll: Den nya husliga arbetsdelningen* [*From the people's home to career households. The new division of domestic labour*], Växjö: Växjö University.

Prout, A. (2005) *The future of childhood: Towards the interdisciplinary study of children*, London: Routledge.

Ridge, T. (2007) 'It's a family affair: Low-income children's perspectives on maternal work', *Journal of Social Policy*, 36(3): 399–416.

Rivas, L.M. (2002) 'Invisible labors: Caring for the independent person', in B. Ehrenreich and A.R. Hochschild (ed) *Global woman: Nannies, maids, and sex workers in the new economy*, London: Granta Books, pp 70–84.

Roberts, D.E. (1997) 'Spiritual and menial housework', *Yale Journal of Law and Feminism*, 9(1): 51–80.

Roman, C. and Peterson, H. (2011) *Familjer i tiden: Förhandling, kön och gränslöst arbete* [*Today's families: Negotiations, gender and limitless labour*], Umeå: Boréa.

Ruddick, S. (1990) *Maternal thinking: Towards a politics of peace*, London: Women's Press.

Samuelsson, T. (2008) *Children's work in Sweden: A part of childhood, a path to adulthood*, Linköping: Linköping University.

Sandin, B. (2012) 'Children and the Swedish welfare state: From different to similar', in P. Fass and M. Grossberg (eds) *Reinventing childhood after World War II*, Philadelphia, PA: University of Pennsylvania Press, pp 110–38.

Sassen, S. (2002) 'Global cities and survival circuits', in B. Ehrenreich and A.R. Hochschild (eds) *Global woman: Nannies, maids, and sex workers in the new economy*, London: Granta Books, pp 254–74.

Schmitz, E. (2007) *Systerskap som politisk handling: Kvinnors organisering i Sverige 1968 till 1982* [*Sisterhood as political action: Women's organisation in Sweden between 1968 and 1982*], Lund: Lund University.

Schwartzman, H.B. (1978) *Transformation: The anthropology of children's play*, New York, NY: Plenum Press.

Sevenhuijsen, S.L. (1993) 'Paradoxes of gender: Ethical and epistemological perspectives on care in feminist political theory', *Acta Politica*, 2: 131–49.

Seymour, J. (2005) 'Entertaining guests or entertaining the guests: Children's emotional labour in hotels, pubs and boarding houses', in J. Goddard (ed) *The politics of childhood: International perspectives, contemporary developments*, Basingstoke: Palgrave Macmillan, pp 90–106.

Sjögren, M. (2003) 'Familjen i servicedemokratin: Ulla Lindström som familjeminister 1954–1966' ['The family in the service democracy: Ulla Lindström as minister of family 1954–1966'], *Socialvetenskaplig tidskrift*, 1: 66–90.

Skeggs, B. (2004) *Class, self, culture*, London: Routledge.

Smart, C. (2007) *Personal life. New directions in sociological thinking*, Cambridge: Polity Press.

Smart, C. (2009) 'Shifting horizons: Reflections on qualitative methods', *Feminist Theory*, 10(3): 295–308.

Smart, C., Neale, B. and Wade, A. (2001) *The changing experience of childhood: Families and divorce*, Malden, MA: Blackwell Publishers.

Sohl, L. (2018) 'Feel-bad moments: Unpacking the complexity of class, gender and whiteness when studying up', *European Journal of Women's Studies*, 25(4): 470–83.

Souralová, A. (2013) *Vietnamese immigrant families and Czech nannies. Mutual dependency, emotionality, and kinship ties in caregiving*, Brno: Masaryk University.

Souralová, A. (2015) *New perspectives on mutual dependency in care-giving*, London: Routledge.

Souralová, A. (2017) 'Children in paid care-giving work: Invisible receivers or active agents in caring relations?', *Childhood*, 24(4): 438–52.

Sparrman, A., Westerling, A., Lind, J. and Dannesboe, K.I. (eds) (2016) *Doing good parenthood: Ideals and practices of parental involvement*, Cham, Switzerland: Palgrave Macmillan.

Spyrou, S. (2009) 'Between intimacy and intolerance. Greek Cypriot children's encounters with Asian domestic workers', *Childhood*, 16(2): 155–73.

Spyrou, S. (2011) 'The limits of children's voice: From authenticity to critical, reflexive representation', *Childhood*, 18(2): 151–65.

Statistics Sweden (2015) 'Mest ROT- RUT-och ränteavdrag till hushåll med höga inkomster' ['ROT and RUT tax deductions are used by high-income households'], www.scb.se/sv_/Hitta-statistik/Artiklar/Mest-skatteavdrag-till-hushall-med-hoga-inkomster/

Statistics Sweden (2016) *På tal om kvinnor och män: Lathund om jämställdhet. 2016 [About women and men: Statistics about gender equality 2016]*, Örebro: Statistiska Centralbyrån.

Stenum, H. (2010) 'Au-pair migration and new inequalities. The transnational production of corruption', in L.W. Isaksen (ed) *Global care work: Gender and migration in Nordic societies*, Lund: Nordic Academic Press, pp 23–48.

Stenum, H. (2015) 'Bane and boon; gains and pains; dos and don'ts ... Moral economy and female bodies in au pair migration', in R. Cox (ed) *Au pairs' lives in global context. Sisters or servants?*, Basingstoke: Palgrave Macmillan, pp 104–20.

Strollo, E. (2013) *Det städade folkhemmet: Tyskfödda hembiträden i efterkrigstidens Sverige [German domestic workers in the 'people's home' of Sweden]*, Linköping: Linköping University.

Stubberud, E. (2015) *Au pairing in Norway. The production of a (non-) worker*, Bergen: Institutt for tverrfaglige kulturstudier, Senter for kjønnsforskning, NTNU.

Swedish Migration Agency (2017) 'Work permits for au pairs', www.migrationsverket.se/English/Private-individuals/Working-in-Sweden/Employed/Special-rules-for-certain-occupations-and-citizens-of-certain-countries/Au-pairs.html

Swedish National Agency for Education (2013) *Föräldrars val och inställning till förskola och fritidshem: resultat från föräldraundersökningen 2012 [Parents choices and attitudes towards daycare and after school care. Results from the parent investigation 2012]*, Stockholm: Skolverket.

Swedish National Agency for Education (2017) 'Barn och personal i förskolan 2017' ['Children and staff in daycare institutions 2017'], www.skolverket.se/publikationer?id=3949

Swedish Tax Agency (2017) 'Rot-och rutavdrag' ['Rot and Rut tax deductions'], www.skatteverket.se/omoss/varverksamhet/statistikochhistorik/skattpaarbete/skattereduktionforrotochrutarbeten.4.3152d9ac158968eb8fd2aa1.html?q=rut+avdrag+2016+summa

Swedish Tax Agency (2018) 'Rutarbeten' ['Rut labour'], www.skatteverket.se/foretagochorganisationer/skatter/rotochrutarbete/rutarbeten.4.2ef18e6a125660db8b080001531.html

Thomson, R. and Holland, J. (2005) '"Thanks for the memory": Memory books as a methodological resource in biographical research', *Qualitative Research*, 5(2): 201–19.

Tronto, J.C. (1993) *Moral boundaries: A political argument for an ethic of care*, London: Routledge.

Tronto, J.C. (1998) 'An ethic of care', *Generations*, 22(3): 15–20.

Tronto, J.C. (2002) 'The nanny question', *Hypatia*, 17(2): 34–61.

Tronto, J.C. (2010) 'The servant problem and justice in households', *Iris: European Journal of Philosophy and Public Debate*, 2(3): 67–85.

Ulmanen, P. (2015) *Omsorgens pris i åtstramningstid: Anhörigomsorg för äldre ur ett könsperspektiv* [*Care in times of austerity: Care for elderly dependants from a gender perspective*], Stockholm: Stockholm University Press.

Ulmanen, P. and Szebehely, M. (2015) 'From the state to the family or to the market? Consequences of reduced residential eldercare in Sweden', *International Journal of Social Welfare*, 24(1): 81–92.

VR (Vetenskapsrådet, Swedish Research Council) (2017) *God forskningssed* [*Good research practice*], Stockholm: Vetenskapsrådet.

Wærness, K. (1984) 'The rationality of caring', *Economic and Industrial Democracy*, 5: 185–211.

Wide, E. (2017) *Att reproducera en människa med hjälp av en annan människa: En affektiv analys av vård- och hemarbete i den privata sfären* [*Reproducing a human being through another human being: An affective analysis of care and housework in the private sphere*], Master's thesis, Helsinki: Helsinki University.

Widmer, E. and Jallinoja, R. (eds) (2008) *Beyond the nuclear family. Families in a configurational perspective*, Bern: Peter Lang.

Wikström, H. (2007) *(O)möjliga positioner: Familjer från Iran & postkoloniala reflektioner* [*(Im)possible positionings: Families from Iran and postcolonial reflections*], Doctoral thesis, Göteborg: Göteborg University.

Wyness, M.G. (2006) *Childhood and society: An introduction to the sociology of childhood*, Basingstoke: Palgrave Macmillan.

Yeates, N. (2012) 'Global care chains: A state-of-the-art review and future directions in care transnationalization research', *Global Networks*, 12(2): 135–54.

Zimmerman, D. and Wieder, D.L. (1977) 'The diary: Diary-interview method', *Journal of Contemporary Ethnography*, 5(4): 479–98.

Index